W9-CIK-146

Issues in University Education

ISSUES IN_____
UNIVERSITY
EDUCATION

ESSAYS BY TEN AMERICAN SCHOLARS

Edited by
CHARLES FRANKEL
Professor of Philosophy,
Columbia University

GREENWOOD PRESS, PUBLISHERS
WESTPORT, CONNECTICUT

70802

Library of Congress Cataloging in Publication Data

Frankel, Charles, 1917-   ed.
    Issues in university education.

    Reprint of the ed. published by Harper, New York.
    1. Education, Higher--Addresses, essays, lectures.
I. Title.
[LB2325.F7 1976]   378.73   76-48978
ISBN 0-8371-9353-2

*All rights in this book are reserved. No part of the book may
be used or reproduced in any manner whatsoever without
written permission except in the case of brief quotations em-
bodied in critical articles and reviews.*

Copyright © 1959 by Harper & Row, Publishers, Inc.

Originally published in 1959 by Harper & Brothers, Publishers,
New York

Reprinted with the permission of Harper & Row Publishers, Inc.

Reprinted in 1976 by Greenwood Press, Inc.

Library of Congress Catalog Card Number 76-48978

ISBN 0-8371-9353-2

Printed in the United States of America

70802

CONTENTS

v

70802

FOREWORD

This book is a cooperative project. It distills the experience of many scholars who have worked and studied in American colleges and universities and who have met together at various places in the United States to discuss the American systems of higher education. The conferences at which these discussions have taken place were financed and sponsored for the first five years by the Hazen Foundation and are now being supported by the Department of State. Most of the scholars who have attended these conferences have been visitors from abroad, who have taken temporary leave from their own universities to come to the United States as visiting professors or research scholars under the joint auspices of the International Educational Exchange Service of the Department of State and their American host institutions. A minority have been Americans, who have had the entertaining, and not infrequently enlightening, experience of trying to explain themselves to others. The contributors to this book have been chosen from this minority. But it is probable that few of them would have written as they have if they had not had the experience of discussion with those who can look on American higher education at least a little from the outside.

Each author, however, is responsible for his own essay alone. Apart from an initial, and very general, assignment of the topics to be discussed by him, each writer has been on his own. No single point of view has been expected, much less imposed, and each contributor has written in his own way on such subjects as seemed to him to be important within the general assignment given to him.

Special acknowledgment should be paid to certain individuals whose names do not appear as contributors. Dr. Elizabeth P. Lam, Dr. Francis A. Young, and Dr. M. H. Trytten of the Committee on International Exchange of Persons of the Conference Board of Associated Research Councils were the moving spirits who originally had the notion that a book like this might be useful. They have spent time and energy in helping, advising, and encouraging the editor and his fellow contributors. Neither they nor the Conference Board of Associated Research Councils are in any way responsible, however, for the contents of this book, which represents only the points of view of the individual authors.

Recognition should also be given to the role played by the Department of State in making this kind of intellectual exchange possible. Under the Smith-Mundt and Fulbright Acts, the Department of State annually sponsors, in cooperation with the governments of other countries, the exchange of approximately 800 American and foreign scholars. The ultimate objective of this exchange is the furthering of mutual understanding between the people of the United States and those of other countries. The conferences on higher education which have developed as a result of this exchange program have provided a unique opportunity for scholars of diverse nationalities and intellectual specialties to meet and discuss common problems, and have given immediate, face-to-face expression to the idea of an international community of scholars.

The role of Mr. Paul Braisted, President of the Edward W. Hazen Foundation, must also be noted with appreciation. It is hoped that this book will offer some permanent testimony to the value of these conferences so generously supported by the Hazen Foundation. Mr. Braisted's own contribution to this book is much greater than the introduction he has kindly consented to write. His good sense and generous spirit have helped every-one who has had the good fortune to be associated with the program in which he has played so large a part.

CHARLES FRANKEL

Columbia University

INTRODUCTION

President
The Edward W. Hazen Foundation

In his *Gitanjali* Rabindranath Tagore has explained the ideal which universities serve as long as they can maintain their independence and integrity. They seek to be places

> Where the mind is without fear and the head is held
>   high;
> Where knowledge is free;
> Where the world has not been broken up into frag-
>   ments by narrow domestic walls;
> Where words come out from the depth of truth;
> Where the clear stream of reason has not lost its way
>   into the dreary desert sand of dead habit. . . .

The university is an embodiment amidst varied and changing social conditions of an unending quest by the mind and spirit of man. The essays gathered in this volume consist of reflections upon this activity as it has taken shape among one people at one moment in their history. But while these essays are focused on American colleges and universities, they speak to needs which are also manifest in other nations, and they grow out of the experience of scholars from many different countries with the American scholarly and educational scene.

It has been the good fortune of American colleges and universities in the postwar era to receive visiting scholars and lecturers in increasing numbers from nearly all parts of the world. Among these visitors have been the Fulbright scholars who have come to lecture in American universities or to carry on their studies in the laboratories and libraries of these institutions. These scholars come from universities that have developed in social circumstances that differ from those in the United States, and it is natural, in the course of their work with American scholars toward common goals, that these scholars should be interested— and sometimes perplexed—by the contrasts they find. Their pre-occupation with the urgent and immediate tasks of teaching and research, however, sometimes deprives them of the opportunity to pursue systematically the questions they have about the purposes and programs of American higher education.

To satisfy the wish such scholars have frequently expressed to explore such questions with other visiting scholars and with American educators, a series of regional conferences for senior Fulbright scholars was first arranged in 1952. These conferences have been organized under the auspices of the Conference Board of Associated Research Councils and with the aid of the Edward W. Hazen Foundation. During the past seven years some 500 visiting scholars and more than 150 American scholars have gathered in twelve regional conferences to explore the meaning of the American experience in higher education. The atmosphere has been informal and candid, and there is abundant evidence that both the Americans and their colleagues from overseas have gained knowledge and insight.

The purpose of these meetings has been threefold. They have given visiting scholars a chance to compare and distill the judgments they have reached as the result of their experience as participants in American higher education. They have given Americans information which can be used in evaluating the exchange program and in improving it. Perhaps most important of all, they have given scholars, whether American, European, African, or Asian, an opportunity to discuss the problems that affect scholarship everywhere at the present moment in history.

The solution of these common problems has usually been the center of discussion, and the American experience has been treated simply as one effort among others to deal with these problems. The rising demands for higher education, the need for scientific and technological knowledge and training, the role of the traditional humanistic disciplines in the midst of rapid social change, the accelerating rate of increase of knowledge, and the need for its wider dissemination: these problems are urgent not only in the United States but among people who are for the first time in full control of their own social institutions as well as in those nations where universities have long been established. These are the problems which have set the broad context in which the discussions of American education have taken place.

It has been thought, therefore, that an interpretation of the American system—or systems—of higher education by representative and respected American scholars who have participated in these conferences would make a further contribution to the continuing discussion of the issues which now loom on the educational horizon in most places in the world. Each scholar has described an aspect of the American university experience and has contributed his own independent reflections on the facts he describes; but he has done so with the interests, needs, and criticisms of scholars from abroad fundamentally in mind. It is probably superfluous to say that the patterns of education in the United States are not offered as models for others. We are more than conscious of our shortcomings. But the interpretations of American higher education which can be found in this volume may have some intrinsic usefulness for those from other countries who visit American institutions of learning, or who are interested in them as social phenomena. These chapters may also suggest issues and problems that press not only on American teachers and scholars, but on teachers and scholars elsewhere in the world.

These essays, then, are fresh reflections upon the American

Issues in University Education

1.

Universities in

the Modern World

RICHARD McKEON
Gray Distinguished Service Professor
University of Chicago

The history of education reflects the history of society and the history of thought. The educational theories and practices of peoples and times are determined by prevailing social relations and values and by available knowledge and attitudes toward its use; and educational systems are, in turn, powerful influences in the development of society and the advancement of knowledge. Periods of social mobility, cultural contacts, and advance in knowledge are periods of educational upheaval. The statement of the interrelations of these interdependent processes of change is somewhat more than a tautology, moreover, since each dimension of change suggests relations and causal influences in the interpretation of the others. Wandering scholars and itinerant professors have always been familiar symptoms of social change, cultural communication, and intellectual upheaval. But at no time in the past has their number approximated the hordes involved in the exchange-of-persons programs instituted during the last decade, and for the first time in history the United States has become one of the centers in educational peregrinations. These phenomena have been the subject of some study: conferences, analyses, and reports have been devoted to what the wanderers seek and do not seek, what they find and do not find, and the accounts of returned scholars have sometimes been

instructive and have often been surprising. But the problems of
the traveler and of the host institution are at once parts and
symptoms of the larger problems of the objectives of universities,
of societies, and of the pursuit of knowledge in the modern
world.

Accounts of educational progress tend to focus on one or another of the dimensions of change: on *what* is taught, as that is
affected by the progress of knowledge or what passes for knowledge; on *who* is taught, as that is affected by social change; on
why that content of knowledge is transmitted to that body of
students under the influence of accepted cultural values and
practical objectives; on *how* it is taught, depending on evolving
professional practices and institutional frameworks and on the
state of knowledge, the aptitude of students, and the hierarchy
of purposes. The circumstances which have fostered changes in
knowledge, social structure, cultural ideals, and educational institutions have usually included increased means of communication among nations, extension of trade, establishment of
relatively safe means of travel, and broadening curiosity. The
wandering scholar has, therefore, been the symbol of changing
circumstances in which training previously unavailable is made
accessible to a new group for purposes newly thought desirable
and with consequences which affect the institutions and life of
distant communities.

The balance between practical and theoretical and between
material and cultural forces has always been delicate in these
interchanges. Periclean Athens was a center which attracted,
for all the reasons that affect educational change, not only
wandering teachers like the Sophists who professed to teach
virtue, rhetoric, and the practical arts, but also Ionian natural
philosophers who became the teachers of Athenian statesmen,
Pythagoreans who combined mathematical and moral teachings
with mystical initiations, poets who wrote of gods and men and

conflicts of loyalties, and artists who transformed the city and were accused of peculation and impiety, as well as men of affairs. The image which we construct of that extraordinary community of men which has had such profound and continuing influence on the education and institutions of Western Europe and Islam must, however, include the forces which led the Athenians to condemn to exile or death many philosophers, statesmen, poets, and artists for whose work Athens was later remembered. In the context of the Roman republic and empire, sons of Romans studied in Greece, but the suspicion continued widespread that the refinements of Greek culture were inconsistent with indigenous Roman virtues, and thus the arts of the Greeks were simplified to practical relevancies in the Roman encyclopedias and oratorical schools.

For a thousand years cultural and intellectual influences were channeled by religious as well as practical purposes. Chinese Buddhists visited the intellectual centers of India; Jewish scholars traveled between Palestine and Babylonia; Islamic religious and legal doctrine, together with classical learning, spread from Arabia and Syria to Persia, to Egypt, and to Spain. The religious traditions influenced each other and came into conflict, and in all the cultural traditions the relation of religious faith to scientific knowledge and secular culture posed problems, while political and dynastic changes sometimes increased communication and sometimes closed borders.

The growth of European universities in the late twelfth and thirteenth centuries was due in part to the increase of available knowledge and in part to the encouragement of emperors, popes, kings, and local communities. Universities were therefore established in the various nations and owed their growth not only to their reputation as centers of studies which attracted scholars but also to the interdictions based on political and religious differences which prevented scholars from traveling. Renaissance humanists traveled in the interest of classical culture, and their voyages had economic, political, and religious implications, while religious reformers and counterreformers set up renewed centers of studies and new programs of education. The progress of science, finally, transformed educational problems and objectives. At the beginning of the nineteenth century British scientists looked to the example of the French École Polytechnique, and at the beginning of the twentieth century American scientists and scholars went to German universities for higher degrees.

The patterns of higher education in all the continents of the world during the second quarter of the twentieth century can be explained only by a complex of interrelated influences: religious and cultural traditions, economic circumstances, international contacts, political aspirations and purposes, and the uses and attractions of knowledge. Against this moving background, the exchange-of-persons program, initiated since the close of World War II, was a massive innovation. It is still only slightly more than ten years old, and it affords a restricted and manageable approach to a complex of educational, social, and intellectual problems. Inquiry concerning that program should throw light on problems focused at both ends of the exchange—on problems of world education and cultural communication and on problems of the functions of a university. The travelers have come for specific educational purposes; their visits have frequently suggested other purposes to them and other functions or perspectives to the institutions they visited. Inquiry into the exchange program, therefore, should not stop at the determination of the extent to which the visitor got what he came for or the extent to which he acquired the facts, attitudes, and skills that the institutions he attended thought he should learn; it should also raise questions about the emerging characteristics of cultural cooperation (when educational exchanges will not center so largely on the training of urgently needed specialists) and about the functions and objectives of universities (in so far as they are affected by new knowledge and new values).

The initial and overwhelming motivations that gave impetus and continuing force to the exchange programs were practical. Practical motivations have been prominent at all stages of educational growth; in all parts of the world and in all times institutions have been established and methods have been constructed to train citizens, preachers, doctors, and lawyers in their tasks. The exchange programs have differed from earlier programs in the scope and diversity of the practical training sought, but not in the fact that they had practical objectives. The "practical" has come to be defined not only by the functions of professions and of citizens but also by the services made available by advances in technology and industry. The great need in many parts of the world at the close of World War II was for technicians and experts in all fields—agriculture, husbandry, forestry, public health, nursing, medicine, social service, engineering, all the varieties of technology, and public and business administration. Viewed from the vantage point of American institutions which participated in the effort to meet these needs, the demands were not surprising, although they were often disconcerting. They were not surprising since they fell precisely in the region in which American educational institutions had made their largest increases in personnel and facilities. Moreover, they corresponded with the interests which have aroused the greatest concern with educational needs during the years since 1945, stimulated by statistics of Soviet accomplishments in producing engineers, in building space missiles, jet planes, and submarines, in constructing major industries, and in increasing the output of consumer goods and agricultural products. They were disconcerting, in part, because the demands of the visitors coincided with local felt needs, and the available facilities were, therefore, soon taxed and overcrowded; and, in part, because they emphasized the distortion resulting from the comparative neglect of the basic studies which give technological skills their foundation and context.

Relatively few of the visiting scholars came to the United States to study the pure or fundamental sciences, the social sciences, or the humanities. Those who did come for this purpose were often inadequately equipped for the work offered in American universities. International contacts have been influential in the exchange of knowledge and the development of methods in fundamental research and cultural understanding in three ways. In the first place, the numerous international meetings of scientists and scholars in all fields have not only contributed to the broadening and deepening of knowledge in particular fields but have also provided influential examples of unbiased communication across borders in which other forms of communication are hampered or blocked. In the second place, scientists and scholars trained abroad have been able to improve training in their home institutions and at once provide substitutes for study abroad and adequate preparation in cases where foreign study is still desirable. Improved courses in the natural sciences, newly established courses in the social sciences, and new techniques in the teaching of languages are among the striking instances of such changes. Finally, the contacts of cultures have accelerated the recognition of the need for broader bases in studies concerned with cultural values—history, literature, philosophy, religion, art, and, in general, cultures and civilizations. This recognition has led in American universities to the increased study of other civilizations—Indian, Islamic, Chinese, Russian, Japanese, Latin American. It has led to the establishment of courses in American culture at some centers of learning abroad.

These are all tendencies which have arisen in response to *ad hoc* needs and to the adjustments they suggest. The practical needs from which they all stem are urgent and not to be denied.

The problem of satisfying them is difficult in itself, but even that problem cannot be treated satisfactorily without considering the questions which it raises with respect to the effects of the vast increase in practical training on the methods and objectives of education in general. The history of thought and education after the Renaissance has sometimes been treated in terms of a conflict between religion and science, and the more recent phases of that history have brought the humanities and the sciences into competition in programs of education and in formulations of cultural objectives. These were at best rough alignments, but even within their limited accuracy and relevance, they have yielded to an alignment in which fundamental research and study in the sciences, the social sciences, the humanities, and religion stand together as a static or declining block in the face of rapidly increasing demands for various forms of practical training.

It is possible to raise these questions, without becoming enmeshed in the complexities of controversies concerning the objectives of education or the structure of knowledge or the ends of life, by reexamining our recent experience to understand the causes underlying the changes we have encountered. Many new problems were faced in the exchange of students and scholars at the end of the war. They were not simply problems of needs created by disorder and destruction but also problems arising out of fundamental economic, social, political, intellectual, and moral changes which were accelerated by the war and by the cumulative influence of these processes on each other. The nations and communities of the world take their individual characters from the stages they have reached; and the relations of peoples and communities to each other are determined by aspirations and frustrations, fears and tensions, that develop from their juxtaposition. An educational exchange program is a response to these environing conditions, and if it is to be assessed from the point of view of the world and its interrelated parts, it must be judged by its contribution to the realization of the aspirations which it is designed to serve.

Economic changes, based on the advancement of science, technology, and industry, have made practicable the aspiration of peoples to satisfy their basic needs, to avoid periodical disasters, epidemics, and famines, to achieve a minimum security in their lives, and, in general, to raise their standards of living. It was natural that educational exchange programs since the close of the war should be used largely to provide technological training. Social changes, accelerated by changes of economic structure, have also made practicable the realization of the aspiration of peoples to share in advantages and goods beyond mere necessities. Programs of basic or fundamental education, extensions of free, universal, compulsory education, campaigns to combat illiteracy, innovations in general education for college students and in adult education for later life, and, in general, efforts to lessen discriminatory disabilities and to increase equality of opportunity have been instrumentalities contributing to this new social fluidity. The accompanying political changes, by which vast numbers acquired the right of self-government, have made practicable the aspiration of peoples to exercise an effective part in decisions affecting their own interests. The accelerating increase in knowledge during the past few centuries, which has laid the foundations of economic, social, and political changes, has made practicable the aspiration of men who previously had benefited only indirectly from scientific advance to share in the accumulated knowledge and make contributions to it. Finally, all these changes have been accompanied by a profound moral revolution, which has yielded a new sense of responsibility, exhibited in international technical assistance programs and in internal efforts to improve the status and opportunities of under-privileged groups, and has made practicable the aspiration of peoples to influence the determination of accepted values and the scope of their distribution.

The emerging importance of universities in the modern world reflects these influences, and the functions universities assume depend on sensitivity to these aspirations and imaginative ingenuity in providing an institutional framework to promote them and to respond to them. The exchange-of-students program provides a useful symptom for diagnosing the problems of universities today. The problems of higher education, like most large practical problems, usually begin as apparently simple problems of providing means for recognized ends and then break through the ambiguous bonds of processes of decision making into moral problems which are not settled by reference to existing structures of value or established measures of equivalence. The new aspirations of peoples have no standard means or measure of satisfaction; they may supplement or hinder each other, and, in particular, the aspiration to satisfy minimum needs may undermine or confuse efforts directed toward social, political, intellectual, and moral values. Misdirection and frustration of any of these aspirations may turn them into forces of retrogression, into new forms of economic, social, or political bondage, and of superstition, ignorance, discrimination, and repression. Among the many institutions in which these aspirations are directed to ends and are provided forms of expression, the universities are strategically located to act in ways which affect numerous and crucial questions of the relation of knowledge to practical action.

The educational exchange programs extend the familiar pattern of wandering scholars into circumstances that give the pattern new dimensions, scope, and potential significance. In the past, the satisfaction of practical needs, determined by established institutions, provided the motive force for the growth and proliferation of universities. The results of education and of the vistas of knowledge opened by inquiry, in turn, modified the conception of the practical and contributed, often in the face of opposition by established powers, to the transformation of power structures, of the social values they served, and of the moral rules they followed. The modern university has become the creature of practical purposes to an extent that overbalances its commitment in the recent past to the advancement and propagation of knowledge and to the study and vitalizing of cultural values. The stress on the practical in educational exchanges has not been limited to the training of technicians and engineers in the strict sense; it has left its impress on all fields. Wandering scholars and international conferences tend to find practical problems in all subjects and therefore to appeal to the expert on problems of population, planning, administration, or cultural relations in the social sciences, on problems of national literary and religious traditions, languages, and philosophical or moral viewpoints in the humanities, and on meteorology, electronics, atomic physics, mathematics, and biochemistry in the natural sciences.

After a decade of educational exchanges, during which the term *exchange* has meant, by and large, the various processes by which the know-how available in some parts of the world has been put at the disposition of other peoples to whom it was not available, the word has come more and more to denote a reciprocal process affecting the institutions, practices, and habits of thought of both participants, and in which express consideration is given not only to the use of knowledge in action but to the effect of practical pressures on our conception and treatment of knowledge. The functions of universities—and of educational exchange programs—is determined by the interplay of the new technology and the new knowledge as they affect emerging economic processes, social values, and moral responsibilities, which in turn condition our attitudes toward needs, preferences, and knowledge.

The basic problems of universities in the modern world take the form of a series of paradoxes. The fundamental paradox is part of the daily experience of those who have participated in international exchange programs: that the objectives and needs of the visitors are fundamentally the same as those of local teachers and students, and that the ways in which the common problems are solved must, nevertheless, continue to be radically different and pluralistic. To fail to recognize that men are everywhere motivated by the same basic aspirations is no less stultifying in educational exchanges than to suppose that the pattern in which aspirations are expressed and pursued by one people will be satisfactory to others. The form of the basic paradox suggests that questions about the functions of universities in the modern world and related questions about educational exchanges, when its primary purpose is cooperative rather than remedial, can be stated accurately and soundly only on the basis of an understanding of the common aspirations of modern men. The dynamic expression of cultural differences can then be found in the balances and interrelations of those aspirations as they appear in changing conceptions of what is desirable and possible and in programs adapted to aspirations so defined. The critical estimation of programs of higher education and the deliberative planning of institutions to carry out improved programs can in turn be adjusted to the calculation of values that must be related if the several aspirations are to take concrete forms and be realized.

The foundation of any structure of values must be the satisfaction of minimum needs; and the revolutionary means to satisfy needs made available by industry and technology has profoundly altered modern theories of value and programs of action. It is still fashionable in some theories to approach all values by way of their economic foundations and prerequisites, but even short of such theoretic dogmas, it is generally recognized that no effective or objective consideration can be given to other values—not even when they are accepted as "higher" values—so long as men are undernourished, weakened by endemic diseases, and insecure. Conversely, it is no less frequently observed that the exigencies and fascinations of the pursuit of necessary material goods can supplant other goods and preclude other interests. Rising standards of living in industrially advanced countries have been accompanied by the development of so-called "materialistic" and "mass" cultures as well as by massive reactions against them; and the efforts of underdeveloped countries to catch up with technological and industrial advances have tended to weaken attachments to traditional values and to increase the temptation to accept economic nostrums which endanger the values associated with human rights, freedom, and dignity.

In the large retrospect of the movements of peoples in the twentieth century, the stirrings of the Chinese people under Sun Yat-sen, of the Indian people under Gandhi, and of the Russian people under Lenin were, for all the differences of cultural values, economic programs, and political ideology which distinguished them, expressions of a hope for new possibilities to relieve misery and to satisfy wants. During the decades between the two World Wars, even before the Soviet Union and the United States emerged from World War II as rival industrial civilizations dedicated to continuing and accelerating technological advance and to assisting and guiding others to acquire its methods and benefits, a very considerable literature had been produced depicting the degradations of the rival "materialisms."[1] The countries of Western Europe gave expression to the paradox by drawing moral lessons from the mass culture and materialistic philosophy consequent on technology, while recognizing that other values and survival itself depended on industrial advance.

[1] See R. McKeon, "Human Values and Technology," *The Conference on Student Life and Education in the United States, June 20–23, 1954* (Chicago: University of Chicago Press, 1955), pp. 36–46, for an exposition for the problem of mass culture and the problem of materialistic philosophy.

The countries in other parts of the world sometimes chose between the two, sometimes vacillated from one image to another, sometimes refused to be forced to a reluctant choice; but the decision was always tempered by a professed hope that they would find their variant from the standard ways to assimilate and to use technology. At each step of economic change, whatever the degree of industrial advancement, decision and policy face numerous, difficult paradoxes: industrial development raises standards of living but requires initial diversion from the production of consumer goods which may lower living standards; increased productivity causes technological unemployment; concentrations of power and capital for development or production restricts individual choice and freedom; ideal consequences anticipated from material advance are postponed by indefinitely increasing appetites for material goods, by oppositions of new interests of new classes, by development of new anxieties and tensions, by invention of new forms of repression and violence, by subordination of other values to manipulations of power and interest, and by search for assurances of self-sufficiency in a world increasingly interdependent.

Universities have been transformed with the changes in society due to technology and the growing aspiration to satisfy basic needs. The function of universities is to increase and transmit knowledge; and that function has come to include an enlarging range of the applications of knowledge as well as somewhat more tentative and puzzled explorations of the implications and consequences of practical changes. The professional schools and even the nonprofessional departments of universities have taken over the training of experts and technologists needed in industry and government. Many new research institutes, community colleges, and regional universities in all parts of the world—in advanced industrial countries and in countries which are turning for the first time to setting up new centers of higher education and to enlarging existing institutions—devote large parts of their programs and budgets to vocational, technical, and practical training. Public concern with education in the United States was widely roused, after years of ineffective efforts to stimulate interest in urgent needs, by reports of the Soviet system of education, which, in turn, had come to attention because of conspicuous successes in the development of space missiles, jet aviation, atomic power, and heavy industry. Plans for the improvement of education in all parts of the world make explicit provisions for the preparation of engineers, technicians, and administrators; and the manpower needs which they project in all the branches of practical services would, if they were ever added into one total, provide employment for a large portion of the world population. But reflections on the bearing of education on the lives of individuals, the amenities of human relations, and the peaceful cooperation of nations are developed in more modest plans and frequently degenerate into platitudes or sophistical propaganda.

Two paradoxes have appeared prominently in the discussion of the uses of knowledge and the predicament of universities. It would seem, if one follows the familiar arguments, that advances in knowledge and control of nature have outrun advances in knowledge of human society and of man, and that excessive concern with the applications of knowledge endangers the continuing basic scientific research, pursued without thought of application in the accumulation of knowledge subject to unsuspected practical applications. In their abstract forms both arguments have received intricate and puzzling elaborations, and there is no agreement concerning the knowledge of values and how it might be applied or the nature of basic research and how it might be encouraged. In the concrete form in which they have affected university planning and practice, the two arguments have led, in the manner of paradoxes, to an acknowledgement that there is something to be said on both sides which can be used to justify any program. Vocational training cannot be separated from education proper, but the aims of liberal education must not be sacrificed.[2] Specialization has tended to break all fields of knowledge into minute parts and to transform inquiry and study into the acquisition of technical knowledge and skills which have no clear relation to each other or to broad practical or cultural applications; but the research scholar and scientist must pursue his own unquestioned way.[3] The experiences of educational exchanges will not resolve the abstract debate nor sharpen the maxims of educational practice, but they do direct attention to the operation of other aspirations which have provided counterbalancing forces to the drive to the practical.

The aspiration of men to goods beyond necessities, to the acquisition, in the phrase of Aristotle, not merely of the bare needs of life, but of what is needed for a good life, grows with success in providing for necessities. The development of economic opportunities has been a source of social change. The universities

[2] Cf. John Grayson, "University Education in Nigeria," *Science and Freedom, A Bulletin of the Committee on Science and Freedom*, no. 12 (October, 1958), p. 35: "I am aware that many university teachers would like to draw a firm distinction between vocational training and education. Nevertheless, even within the cloistered shade of the oldest universities the direction of modern life is such that the two can no longer be separated. In my view there is nothing at all to be ashamed of in the fact that this college aims to produce not merely good conversationalists, but young men and women fitted in all ways to contribute positively to society. Nevertheless, the aims of any university must always be wider than the mere mass production of doctors, teachers, scientists, and civil servants. If our graduates are to emerge with breadth of vision and well developed critical faculties, it is vital that fundamental standards of scholarship should be preserved."

[3] Cf. M. L. Oliphant, quoted in George F. Kneller, *Higher Learning in Britain* (Berkeley: University of California Press, 1955), p. 201: "A University is not a static foundation, but one which absorbs, by an evolutionary process, the best of the results of all serious experiments in higher education. In my view the experiment of the nineteenth century, which introduced the complex divisions of engineering and applied science to the universities, has been a failure, whereas the growth of the fundamental sciences has added to their stature."

and the Church were important sources of social fluidity in the Middle Ages. The universities served a like function in the United States in the nineteenth and early twentieth centuries by providing an opportunity for immigrants of all classes to satisfy their ambition, often at great sacrifice, to educate their children. The problem of a more diversified undergraduate body led in the twentieth century to the development of "general education": experiments after World War I at centers like Amherst, Columbia, and Chicago with general courses in the social sciences, the humanities, the natural sciences, the great books, the study of cultures; elaboration of methods, objectives, and theories in the thirties; and, finally, conferences and the publication of reports in the forties.

Since higher education is no longer the perquisite of the young of the privileged classes alone, college students can no longer be presumed to have a common cultural background or intellectual preparation. The question, "What should an educated man know?" has several dimensions. His education should reflect the state of knowledge and contemporary problems more closely than the presumed common culture of an elite did in the past. It should, therefore, take into account the conception of the world developed by science and the influence of scientific ways of thought, the operation and history of social and political institutions and the judgment required for their effective operation, the values expressed in art, philosophy, and religion, and the perceptive appreciation that opens up their significance. General education, moreover, has a bearing on other problems of education, including problems of the nature and methods of technical training and of preparation for citizenship, research, and morality. General education, finally, has a world dimension: if it is truly general, it should be what educated men should know in all parts of the world, and what that is will be determined only by consultation and cooperation of men from all parts of the world.

afford; others argued that general education properly conceived contributed directly to the formation of effective experts. The debates had a familiar sound to anyone who had taken part in the early stages of American planning for general education. It is safe to predict that many forms of general education will evolve, adapted to the institutions and needs of different communities, and that international cooperation will serve a double function—in clarifying the common objectives to which general education is directed, and in developing variant means by which the practice of general education may be improved and broadened.

The aspiration of peoples to take an effective part in decisions which affect their interests and welfare has found new channels of realization as a result of economic and social changes. During the decade or more since the end of World War II, hundreds of millions of people who lived formerly in colonial status or under other forms of dependence and tutelage, foreign or domestic, have acquired the right of self-government and of determination of their own affairs. Yet the use and preservation of that right has faced extreme difficulties. Newly established democratic institutions have been strained by the pressing urgency of economic problems; in the absence of informed, alert, and educated bodies of citizens, democratic institutions have provided new and massive sources of corruption or have necessitated the restrictions of "guided democracy"; the transformation of new and old democracies into military despotisms has been kaleidoscopic; the conditions of free and well-grounded choice have often disappeared, and nations have been brought by force and propaganda under the dominance of dictatorships which often preserve the language of democracy, but merge it with the idiom of paternalism and with coercive institutions imimical to free debate and discussion.

Education has an essential function in the development of democracy: it must not only promote literacy and make information available, but it must also arouse interest, establish attitudes, and promote mutual understanding, confidence, insight, and awareness of common interests. The Indian *Report of the University Education Commission* devotes a chapter to the Aims of University Education. This contains a brief but profound analysis of the relation of education to democracy, justice, liberty, equality, fraternity, and the continuity of Indian culture. These are problems which the exchange programs have entered into only tangentially, but their implications are inescapable in the modern world. Among other things, the ideals of democracy and the operation of democratic institutions are not as clear as they might be made even to the citizens of countries which have had a long experience of democracy; and we have failed to communicate the meaning of that experience or the arts and virtues on which democracy depends to people who are attracted by democratic ends but puzzled by democratic processes. We have criticized the undemocratic practices and the violations of rights and liberties in the "people's democracies," but we have not made the classics of Western democracy or statements of its theory and practice widely available, despite the obvious need for them. In 1957 UNESCO compiled a list of the world's most translated authors during the period 1948–1955.[6] Lenin headed the list with 968 translations, Stalin was third (separated from Lenin by the Bible), Marx was tenth, Engels eleventh. There was no Western writer on political, social, or economic theory and practice on the list of 101 authors. It is not easy to educate people for democracy, and it is not easy to set forth the conditions and problems of democracy in the twentieth century. Yet the people of the world must be given the means to understand what is involved in their present choices, and it is the responsibility of universities to promote that understanding. The problem cannot be understood and action cannot be effective on less than a world-

[6] *The UNESCO Courier* (February, 1947), p. 8.

wide scale, and both theory and practice are advanced by the experiences and insights of international exchanges.

The realization of the aspiration of people, not only to share in the benefits of scientific and cultural advances, but also to participate in them and contribute to them, falls most directly within the province of the university. Universities are institutions of learning and teaching, of research and education; and indeed it is by amassing and transmitting knowledge that they contribute to the satisfaction of needs, the achievement of a good life, and the control of one's own destiny. But the four purposes are independent as well as interrelated, and the higher learning will lose its function unless the facilities of scholarship and free research are guarded and maintained at a high level. The advancement of knowledge may be hindered by the limitations of narrow views of the useful and the practical, by the rigidities of cultural traditions, or by the repressions of political control.

Communication and cooperation have important contributions to make in preserving and strengthening the conditions of free inquiry. The free exchange of knowledge is at once the means by which knowledge is advanced, the source of judgment by which it is weighed, and the stimulus to interest by which it is encouraged. Freedom, facilities, criteria, and interest are the interrelated conditions required for the advance of knowledge, and among them freedom is the indispensable beginning. Scholarly and scientific communication and educational exchanges are forces for advancing freedom. The problem of facilities varies from field to field: it is easier to tabulate the items of equipment needed in a laboratory or the list of books that constitutes a good research library than to specify such less tangible facilities as the challenge of fellow workers and recognized standards, or the inspiration of continuing interest ranging from adequate media of publication to the recognition of an informed larger public. The short cuts which depend on abandoning freedom in organizing the advance in knowledge are as illusory as the royal roads to knowledge; and the universities of the world are among the major factors in that diversified advancement of knowledge which is the basis of technology and technical training, of insight into values and meanings, and of development of democratic institutions and attitudes.

The economic, social, political, and intellectual changes which have formed the modern world to which the university must adjust and to which it must make its contribution have been accompanied by a profound moral revolution which is an expression of the aspiration to realize and recognize the claims of human dignity and integrity. The moral revolution is involved in the most tangled forms of the paradoxes of modern change. It is the object of attention primarily at festive academic celebrations, interdisciplinary seminars, or interchurch conferences; it is invoked during political campaigns, ideological analyses, and international crises. It has taken the form of a new sense of responsibility[7] exhibited in international assistance programs and in internal efforts to improve the status and opportunities of underprivileged groups. But it has, moreover, developed contemporaneously with the most highly organized programs of discrimination, suppression, and liquidation, and the most effective programs of mendacious and misleading propaganda that the world has ever seen.

Guidance of responsible action has been sought alternatively, in these violently confused circumstances, in hopes that sciences of man and human action will be developed, that an economic or political system will triumph, that a new humanism will be created, or that religion will be revitalized. The experience of educational exchanges has had a modest contribution to make to

[7] Cf. R. McKeon, "The Development and the Significance of the Concept of Responsibility," *Revue internationale de philosophie* No. 39 (1957), pp. 3–32 (Entretiens de Paris, 1956).

70807

these massive problems. Exchange programs operate on the assumption that responsibility means communication and reciprocation and that reciprocity involves an interchange of four kinds: (1) recognition that the values of men are determined by needs and interests and acceptance therefore of the basic convictions of others; (2) concern with the distribution of values and provision that the pursuit of values by any person or group will not lessen the opportunity of others to pursue like values; (3) rational adjustment of interests and common goods to limitations and specifications of facts and circumstances; and (4) cooperation in the maximization of values in individual lives and cultural patterns. Irresponsibility takes various forms, including exclusive concern with private interests or the special interests of particular groups, arbitrary imposition of value preferences and systems on others, insidious propaganda which takes advantage of needs and misstates facts and possibilities, and one-sided distortions and limited degradations of values. Universities combat irresponsibility by promoting knowledge and understanding.

International educational exchange programs have thus far concentrated largely on practical problems. In the emerging forms in which the treatment of international problems of higher education and the higher learning will center more and more in the universities and learned institutions in the various parts of the world and in communication and cooperation among them, the problems of exchanges will continue in a profound sense to be practical. But they will no longer be only the urgent problems of training technicians and experts critically needed. The task of training and of education is being taken over more and more by local institutions available to students in all parts of the world. It is time to turn attention to related but larger practical problems which are the proper province of universities since they depend directly on knowledge and the use of knowledge in the service of values: problems of how the potentialities of individ-

70802

uals may best be developed, how the values of communities may be discovered and realized, how men may come to agreement in common action and policy, how the advancement of knowledge may be promoted, and how the dignity of man may be made a concrete objective of moral action rather than a phrase for edification or deceit. The functions of universities embrace economic needs, cultural values, political policies, scientific and scholarly knowledge, and moral wisdom. The wandering of scholars should contribute to the formulation of common problems and to the discovery of common truths rather than simply to the satisfaction of curiosity concerning the odd ways other people do things which we do differently or to the confirmation of prejudices and stereotypes concerning alien errors, illusions, and depravities. Our international problems assume a practical turn because we are already living in a world community of interrelated needs and interdependent resources. They will continue to be practical problems, even on this initial level, only if we can find solutions to them which also contribute to the development of freedom, fraternity, democracy, equality, and wisdom in the community of nations and peoples. It is a problem which will require learning, insight, and tact, for its treatment depends on relating a radical pluralism—of attitudes, motives, cultural values, beliefs, political programs, intellectual theories and hypotheses—to common values and to communication about them. The universities of the world must make a crucial contribution to this problem, and they will take on new forms and functions as they explore it and follow through its implications.

2.

The American University
and Changing Philosophies
of Education

ROBERT ULICH
Professor of Education
Harvard University

American colleges and universities are a part of the totality
of Western higher education. Their tasks and problems reflect
the tasks and problems with which Western civilization, and in
one form or another all humanity, has been confronted in its
endeavor to widen and deepen man's knowledge about himself
and the universe in which he lives. In this essay I shall attempt
to relate American higher education to certain episodes in the
history of Western scholarship and to certain issues which have
emerged in that history. For we must understand this background if we wish to understand the present situation.

I

Although the remark is half facetious, there is still some
justification in saying that there has rarely been a society so
quick to be disloyal to its own principles as the historical society
of academic scholars. Scholars have a reputation for conservatism;
but the word is a weak one to describe the reality.

Examples of this sad truth are recurrent. It took centuries
of slow cultural maturation until European Christianity was
ready to build the medieval scholastic university of Albert of
Cologne, Thomas Aquinas, and Duns Scotus. But less than two
hundred years after the middle of the thirteenth century, which

24

is the time when St. Thomas wrote his great *Summae*, the decline
of the scholastic university was already apparent. Though still
thinking within the framework of the Christian heritage, the
learned *doctores* disagreed about almost every point that allowed
for differences of opinion, and especially about the relationship
between divine reason, or revelation, on the one hand, and
human reason, or autonomous rationality, on the other hand—
a central problem for the unity of the tradition. For some
theologians, apparently, Aristotle had become a greater teacher
than Christ. Inevitably, they accused one another of heresy. In
addition, the examination system became venal; and the moral
conduct of many teachers and students was scandalous.

Again, in the fifteenth and sixteenth centuries, the humanists
and the religious reformers protested against the corruption and
barrenness of the "monkish learning." But the humanists soon
mistook the imitation of Cicero's style for intellectual and
esthetic productiveness; and it is only with a feeling of sadness
that one can compare what the Protestant universities were really
like at the end of the sixteenth and during the seventeenth centuries with the ideas which Luther and Calvin had cherished
about Christian learning.

During the seventeenth and eighteenth centuries still again,
when scientific empiricism and rationalism changed traditional
patterns of thought, many of the famous universities remained
aloof, not understanding the importance of the methods and
criteria of research that had slowly arisen within their own ranks.
Of course, the North-Italian universities tried to protect Galileo
from ecclesiastical persecution, and two generations later Newton
taught at Cambridge. The Dutch universities as well—the
Netherlands being then the haven of political and intellectual
refugees—allowed their scholars some amount of freedom. However, they never invited or even protected Spinoza, the great
Jewish philosopher, who in the introduction to his *Tractatus*

Theologico-Politicus (1670) asked for *libertas philosophandi*
(liberty of thought) as the prerequisite to finding one's way to
both truth and God. And like him, many of the outstanding
minds of the seventeenth and eighteenth centuries either did not
want, or for reasons political, intellectual, or religious were
given no chance, to teach at a university. They include Comenius,
Descartes, Huygens, Locke, Leibnitz, Voltaire, Diderot, d'Alembert. Hume, accused of heresy, failed to secure a professorial
chair at Edinburgh; all he could obtain was the position of
librarian of the Advocate's Library in his home town. The University of Paris, in the thirteenth and fourteenth centuries the
most famous and the most international of universities, harbor-
ing scholars from almost all Catholic countries, with native
Frenchmen only a small minority, had, after the fifteenth century, succumbed to the grip of monarchical and ecclesiastical reaction. From the sixteenth century on, it missed every opportunity
to maintain its reputation by lending its prestige to new movements, until, during the decades before the revolution of 1789, it
had become the symbol of mental slavery, though situated in a
city that vibrated with intellectual energy.

During these centuries of decline of the older institutions, it
was the scientific "Academies" in Italy, France, England, and
Germany that provided the opportunity for free communication
of ideas. Many of the great men of Europe corresponded with
the Royal Society of London. Comenius dedicated to it his
Via Lucis (Way of Light), and Frederick the Great of Prussia
offered the presidency of the Academy of Berlin several times
to the French mathematician d'Alembert. Enlightened statesmen of the time despaired of the universities ever again becoming centers of intellectual vitality and comprehension. They
thought of dividing them into separate professional schools.

It was then that the absolute princes of the states of Germany
began to think of their universities as instruments by which to

advance the progress and prestige of their relatively small countries. Halle, Goettingen, and finally the University of Berlin, founded in 1810, began to bring into being what Spinoza had dreamed of. They became centers of scholarly freedom—within limits, of course, but nevertheless with wider opportunities for unhampered inquiry than had heretofore existed.

Such essays as those written by the liberal theologian Schleiermacher, the philosopher Fichte, and the scientist Steffens about the spirit of the true university,[1] elevate the idea of higher education far beyond the low level of the preceding centuries. They represent perhaps the finest essays ever written about both the mission of universities as the associations of freely inquiring men and the obligation of the modern state to support these associations in the interest of the liberty of its citizens and its own internal and external welfare. Nevertheless, with the exception of Steffens, these thinkers did not foresee the role which the natural sciences were going to play in the future. Like Wilhelm von Humboldt, the leading spirit behind the reform of Prussian education after the defeat by Napoleon, they represented philosophical idealism pure and proper and gave the humanities the central place among the disciplines. Even Steffens, a Norwegian by birth, who, as professor of physics at the universities of Breslau and Berlin, corrected some of the aprioristic speculations about nature indulged in by the leading systematizers of his time, still thought of the natural sciences too much as a branch simply of philosophy.

But philosophical idealism was still more shortlived than theological scholasticism. For it took only a few decades until the humanities in the German universities found a powerful

---

[1] *Über das Wasen der Universität. Drei Aufsätze von Joh. Gottl. Fichte, Friedrich Schleiermacher, Henrik Steffens aus den Jahren 1807–1809.* Mit einer Einleitung über "Staat und Universität" herausgegeben von Eduard Spranger. Neue Ausgabe (Leipzig: Felix Meiner, 1919).

competitor in the exact sciences. The influence which German scholarship exercised over the universities of other countries during the period between the Napoleonic Wars and World War I was due at least as much to its excellence in the natural sciences as in the humanities.

II

The nation which during this era most eagerly absorbed German learning was the United States of America. Its early colleges, Harvard, William and Mary, and Yale were founded on the conviction that the best way to build up a Christian civilization on the new continent was to teach the Protestant religion together with the classical languages, including Hebrew, the language of the Old Testament. Even when, at the beginning of the eighteenth century, the enlightenment pushed the old theological hierarchy to the defensive, the program of study in American colleges did not change considerably.

There were, of course, dissenting voices and institutions. Benjamin Franklin's pragmatic and utilitarian spirit influenced the College, Academy, and Charity School of Philadelphia, which was chartered in 1755 and developed later into the University of Pennsylvania. No religious urge motivated the sponsors; they were interested in both the "most useful" and the "most ornamental" learning (the latter term one that had already been used by Locke and his friends to designate the classical studies). On the initiative of Thomas Jefferson, the Assembly of Virginia passed in 1786 an Act for Establishing Religious Freedom that began, "Well aware that Almighty God hath created the mind free; that all attempts to influence it by temporal punishments or burdens, or by civil incapacitations, tend only to beget habits of hypocrisy and meanness. . . ." Naturally, the same Jefferson could not but disapprove of the parochial spirit of the American colleges. Though himself an accomplished classicist, as his beautiful letters reveal, he nevertheless propagated a wider program of higher education, better adapted to his time. The University of Virginia, founded in 1825 under his auspices, gave the students a choice of any one of eight "schools," devoted not only to the humanities, but also to law and the sciences. There was no department of divinity.

More and more the settlers of the new continent became reluctant to submit to the dictatorship of the old European tradition. But in 1827 Yale, then the college most respected by the conservatives (Harvard had already disappointed them on several occasions) saved for some further decades the dominance of the old and venerated academic tradition. Theology, to be sure, had already receded. But in a language breathing the dignity of a great conviction, the Yale faculty pleaded for the preservation of the classics, philosophy, mathematics, and the sciences as a unity that could not be divided into specialized parts without destroying the western ideal of the educated man.[2] According to the Yale professors, a psychological or pedagogical reason could also be given for the preservation of the liberal arts. This was the now generally discarded "faculty psychology" or theory of "mental discipline." "The two great points to be gained in intellectual culture, are the *discipline* and the *furniture* of the mind; expanding its powers, and storing it with knowledge. The former of these is, perhaps, the more important of the two." Accordingly, the faculty expressed itself against the mere accumulation of facts or the too early training in utilitarian and professional subjects. "Professional studies are designedly excluded from the course of instruction at college to leave room for those literary and scientific acquisitions which, if not commenced there, will, in most cases, never be made."

[2] *Reports of a Course of Instruction in Yale College by a Committee of the Corporation and the Academical Faculty* (New Haven: Hezekiah Howe, 1828). Reprinted in the *American Journal of Science and Arts*, 15, 1828.

But unfortunately—or fortunately, depending on one's stand-point—for only a few decades could the colleges be kept within the educational philosophy of the Yale report. The spirit of Franklin, Jefferson, and several other rebels, pushed back for a while, began to reassert itself with increasing vigor. It had on its side the scientific, technical, and industrial development of the Western nations, together with the rapid expansion of the comparative and international studies which accompanied the widening of communications among the peoples of the world. Whatever the merits of the older "genteel" tradition, it could no longer be considered an end in itself; its value had to be judged relatively to other values. Here American colleges simply followed a trend that had shown its inescapable power in the universities of Old Europe. For there, too—though at a different speed—the old *globus intellectualis*, mirroring essentially the Greek-Roman-Christian heritage, proved to be incommensurate with the expanse of new knowledge, new ideas, and emerging professions.

Now it was Harvard's turn. President Charles W. Eliot, after returning from a study of the new European trends in higher education, became professor of chemistry at the new Massachusetts Institute of Technology and taught also at Harvard. He insisted on laboratory work, demanded written examinations, and did almost everything in his power to disturb the comfortable peace on which so many of his associates—following an old and venerated custom—laid apparently more value than on progress in scholarship. To the displeasure of many of Eliot's colleagues, the overseers of Harvard elected him president in 1869.

With admirable courage Eliot immediately stated the principles of his policy in the inaugural address which has become so famous.[3]

---

[3] Charles W. Eliot, "Inaugural Address," delivered on October 19, 1869. In Charles W. Eliot, *The Man and His Beliefs*, ed. William Allan Neilson. Vol. I (New York: Harper and Brothers, 1926).

The endless controversies whether language, philosophy, mathematics, or science supplies the best mental training, whether general education should be chiefly literary or chiefly scientific, have no practical lessons for us today. This university recognizes no real antagonism between literature and science, and consents to no such narrow alternatives as mathematics or classics, science or metaphysics. We should have them all, and at their best. To observe keenly, to reason soundly, and to imagine vividly are operations as essential as that of a clear and forcible expression; and to develop one of these faculties, it is not necessary to repress and dwarf the others.

What Eliot had observed in Germany happened at Harvard. The university professor was no longer supposed to be the preacher of supposedly established verities but the leader in the search for truth, wherever and however it could be found. In order to carry his ideas into practice, Eliot gradually instituted the so-called system of electives, allowing a student the freedom to choose the courses he considered most suited to his interests and talent. "The vulgar argument"—so he answered the followers of the Yale report of 1828—"that the study of the classics is necessary to make a gentleman is beneath contempt."

Despite considerable opposition from the conservative forces led by Yale and Princeton, the influence of Harvard was great and stimulating. It made the American colleges aware of the fact that, some excellent teachers notwithstanding, they had been more a glorified form of secondary school than real institutions of higher education. It forced them to change teaching methods from memorization to active understanding; and finally it led them to become comprehensive universities by building graduate schools over and above the undergraduate college. Johns Hopkins in Baltimore, Clark University in Worcester, and the Catholic University of Washington were initially organized solely as graduate universities, thus transplanting the German example to American soil. And as the new type of

German university had been inspired by the philosophy of idealism, so Eliot's scheme received a kind of higher sanction by
Darwinism. The "evolutionary process," the "survival of the
fittest," "natural selection"—since these events occurred in
nature, why should not man, who, after all, is a part of nature,
follow the same laws of life in his struggle for progress?

But however much productive energy was released by the
elective system, the system also had its flaws. Together with an
atomization and superabundance of course offerings, it allowed
students such a measure of early specialization that the degree of
communication of ideas necessary among educated people was en-
dangered. In addition, after about 1890 the American high
school (or secondary school) also changed its character rapidly.
It became no longer a selective, college-preparatory school,
generally comparable to the French Lycée or the German
Gymnasium, but changed rapidly into an institution for citizenship education, sending to the colleges an ever-growing number
of students who were often ill prepared, who did not know what
to do with their academic freedom, and who made a potpourri
of easily digestible subjects out of their elective program of
studies.

Thus, during the first decade of the twentieth century, exactly
at the time when the nineteenth century's philosophical and
social applications of Darwinism also came more and more under
fire, the elective system was seriously reexamined. At Harvard
itself, President Abbott Lawrence Lowell challenged the policy
of his predecessor. He did not abolish it, but he required freshmen and sophomores (students in the first and second years of
college) to select courses from groups of subjects that were supposed to combine a certain variety with an inner unity; at the
same time, however, he permitted "concentration" or specialization to juniors and seniors (students in the third and fourth
years).

Again college after college followed Harvard's lead. The Cassandra warnings of Yale and Princeton when they had opposed Eliot's program were recalled. "Distribution" and "concentration" now became the fashionable scheme. But the critics and policy makers did not stop there. From highly diverse points of view they attacked what they considered the "pompous vulgarity," "aimless profusion," "lack of tradition," "mass production," "cafeteria system," "anti-intellectualism," and "course-credit-veneration" of the American university.[4] Behind this change of climate there was not only the American tendency to swerve quickly from veneration to criticism—as is vividly illustrated by the changing prestige of John Dewey's philosophy during the first half of this century—but deeper reasons as well. The source of this unrest in American education can be found in what is known as "the crisis of our time," a phrase which is now used so often that one forgets that there never was a productive period in the history of mankind that did not have its crisis. What are the elements of this crisis that affect the philosophy of higher education?

III

1. At the end of World War I, President Wilson's program envisaged a reform of the European political system and a world made "safe for democracy," a world where doors would be opened to free and experimental, instead of authoritarian, forms of living. Unhappily, many of the peoples of the world became neither democratic nor peace-loving, but communist, fascist,

---

[4] See Dietrich Gerhard, "The Emergence of the Credit System in American Education considered as a Problem of Social and Intellectual History," *Bulletin of the American Association of University Professors*, 41, 1955, No. 4. For the most serious criticism of American higher education before World War II, see Abraham Flexner, *Universities. American, English, German* (New York: Oxford University Press, 1930). See also Horace Kallen, *College Prolongs Infancy* (New York: The John Day Company, 1932).

nationalist, or simply rebellious. They "experimented," but, from the American point of view, in the wrong direction. In the United States, accordingly, the view developed that there was a fallacy in the prevailing American philosophy of history, a mistaken assumption that progress would be the natural result of the process of trial and error, in politics as well as in education. Suddenly, instead of looking confidently toward the future, many of the sophisticated looked nostalgically toward the past, toward stability rather than toward change, toward peace of mind rather than toward continuous risk. One consequence was a moderate renaissance of medieval studies in America. For the Middle Ages were supposed to have given the soul of man the inner felicity of which he is deprived today, though, when seriously studied, that period reveals just as severe and cruel inner conflicts as does our own troubled age, and at the same time many other characteristics, such as poverty, filth, illiteracy, intolerance, parochialism, slavery, and tryanny, which today are no longer considered to be a part of divine dispensation but evils possible of correction.

2. This changed attitude toward the meaning of history has caused a certain, though perhaps not too serious, flirtation with Catholicism in academic circles; and in any case there has certainly been awakened a new interest in religion. Books by Jacques Maritain (Catholic), Sir Walter Moberley, and Arnold S. Nash (Protestant) were, and still are, widely discussed.[5] It is perhaps a mark of this new trend that, after a succession of rather secularly minded administrators, the Harvard Corporation in 1953 appointed a president of avowed religious convictions.

3. Naturally, the humanists have also appeared among the

[5] Jacques Maritain, *Education at the Crossroads* (New Haven: Yale University Press, 1943). Sir Walter Moberley, *The Crisis in the University* (London: SCM Press, 1949). Arnold Samuel Nash, *The University and the Modern World: An Essay in the Philosophy of University Education* (New York: The Macmillan Company, 1943).

edition of the so-called "Hundred Great Books," selected to present to the reader those classical works on whose wisdom, allegedly, human civilization is built. Many objections have been raised against this enterprise. The selection has been character- ized as biased; it has rightly been said that if swallowed whole- sale by an inexperienced reader the Hundred Books could create more confusion than enlightenment; and it has also been pointed out that they contain many ideas which, though histori- cally important, are today outdated. In spite of these criticisms the books are used in many colleges and adult discussion groups, and they have, at least to a degree, succeeded in giving a pri- marily pragmatic people a better sense of historical continuity. However, the hope that the program of St. John's College in Annapolis, based on Hutchins's concept of the study of the liberal arts as a coherent sequence of great events in the history of hu- man reason, might start a widening movement in American undergraduate education has not been realized. St. John's Col- lege stands alone and has not considerably enlarged the number of its students. Evidently, classicism—particularly of this variety —does not appeal to the American mind. This remark, I hope, will not be misunderstood. I personally believe in the irreplace- able value of the classical studies because I am convinced that a culture that wants to develop and at the same time preserve its identity has to be conscious of its roots. In addition, I believe that the beauty of the Greek and Latin languages is such that it should be made available to perceptive minds. But I have no illusions about the fact that the enormous increase of knowledge in our time will relegate the classical tongues to an increasingly minor role in modern education. The great question is how to replace them. We shall have to work with translations. But experience teaches us that translations lose in meaning and will easily be neglected unless there are a sufficient number of people who can interpret them on the basis of their knowledge of the original sources and of the culture in which they originated.

But whatever our opinions about this point, the conviction has grown that without serious reforms the American college will lose the purpose it has set for itself—liberal education. Situated as it is in between the high school, a type of middle school which has accepted more and more social responsibilities at the expense of strictly academic ones, and graduate schools with a definite obligation to give professional training, the college will always have to navigate precariously between the Scylla of providing superficial information about everything and anything and the Charybdis of encouraging too early specialization for later graduate studies.

The realization of this danger caused Columbia University to introduce, right after World War I, an obligatory course in contemporary civilization, intended to explain to the student the significant features and issues of the present by showing their relation to the great history-forming events of the past. Subsequently, Columbia also introduced a required course in classics of Western literature and philosophy, although the philosophy of this course was different from that of Chancellor Hutchins. The same purpose also motivated the Harvard faculty to publish the Harvard report on *General Education in a Free Society*,[8] issued under the presidency of James Bryant Conant. According to this scheme, which is in essence a reorganization of President Lowell's plan of distribution and concentration, every student is required to take six of his total sixteen undergraduate courses in the area of "general education." One course in the social sciences, one in the humanities, and one in the natural sciences are obligatory requirements in the first year. The remaining general courses can be taken at any time before grad-

---

[8] *General Education in a Free Society*. Report of the Harvard Committee. With an Introduction by James Bryant Conant (1st ed., 1945; 15th printing, 1955, Cambridge: Harvard University Press).

uation so that the student is, so to speak, compelled to combine his desire for preprofessional preparation with a broader view of the intellectual landscape. Thus, the Harvard report on general education and the college plan created at Chicago under the auspices of President Hutchins aim at providing a minimum of cultural and educational unity within the bewildering diversity of modern specialized interests. The Harvard report also includes—and here is one of the reasons for its amazingly wide popularity—a discussion of the problems created for higher education by the complicated nature of the American high school, so totally different from the secondary schools which in other countries prepare the adolescent for his later academic responsiblities.

But while today most American colleges attempt to acquaint the student, during the first years of study, with the common foundations of our highly complex civilization, a minority of educators, influenced by "progressive education," deplore the uniformity, the large classes, and the consequent lack of individuality in our colleges. They also deplore the absence of attention to the esthetic and active components in the education of youh toward maturity. Regarding these various concerns they could find support in the findings of the so-called Hazen report on *Changing Values in College*[9] which proves that too many students remain, as it were, strangers to the intellectual and ethical values of the academic world. They study partly because it is a path to professional advancement and better living, partly because college attendance, rather than being a privilege, has become a kind of social convention among the middle classes. It seems that among these progressive-individualistic institutions Sarah Lawrence, Bennington, and Goddard have conquered a

[9] *Changing Values in College: An Exploratory Study of the Impact of General Education in Social Sciences on the Values of American Students,* by Philip E. Jacob (New York: Harper & Brothers, 1957).

permanent place in American higher education. And it is certainly not accidental that, while Goddard is coeducational, the first two are institutions for women, for many people, who do not think the old question of the equality of the sexes is any longer worth debating, may nevertheless (or perhaps for this very reason) ask themselves whether women's colleges, instead of imitating colleges for men, might make a unique contribution to human civilization by more boldly asserting the cultural qualities of womanhood.

IV

Looking back at this brief history of higher education we may ask: Is there a deeper philosophy inherent in all these changes, or are they merely adjustments to environmental conditions? Or we may ask: Is the increasing variety in universities and in the educational policy of our colleges due to principled action, or are they merely signs of increasing confusion?

Certainly, external factors, not directly inherent in the pursuit of learning as such, have played their role. The great universities of Western civilization, from Paris, Bologna, Oxford, and Cambridge to the German and the modern American universities, could not remain unaffected by the many, often too many, interests they were expected to serve. All over the world, universities educate youth today not merely for disinterested scholarship or for the old "three higher faculties" of theology, law, and medicine, built on top of the faculty of the *artes liberales,* but for a constantly widening number of professions; and the professions impose their demands. The enormous range of the applied sciences, from engineering, radiology, and modern metallurgy to economics and industrial management could not be foreseen even a hundred years ago. Radio, television, electronics did not exist. The old humanities have split into innumerable subdivisions and the social sciences have made themselves independent. Our institutions of higher learning have become increasingly expensive, and whether the money comes from private donors or from the government, in either case influences may be exerted which are alien to the true nature of intellectual search. Every society wishes its future leaders, teachers, and officials to support its ideals, perhaps also its prejudices and nationalist aspirations; and in more than one case universities have become instruments of power groups rather than clearing houses in the strife of parties.[10] A mind with a negativistic bent could write a devastating story about the voluntary or involuntary slavery of university professors. They have sometimes been terribly disloyal to their professed principles and the genuine spirit of their institutions. Scholars are human, often all too human; they form cliques, they have vested interests, they are often ridiculously interested in privileges and honors. Many of them have been bribed, sometimes even without their knowing it. And why should they be the only mortals who are not confused when confronted with the complexities and contradictions in human life?

Yet there is also some greatness in the picture. The truly decisive changes and movements in the history of higher education have not been caused by pressure from the outside or by timidity and intellectual disloyalty from the inside. Rather they have been caused by the fact that universities are the living incorporations and symbols of man's insatiable thirst for truth. And though the final and ultimate truth is beyond the reach of fallible human reason, this reason has nevertheless the *vision* of a goal, which is to eliminate error and illusion, and to come closer to that which *really* is. The pursuit of such a goal requires the

[10] See Richard Hofstadter and Walter P. Metzger, *The Development of Academic Freedom in the United States* (New York: Columbia University Press, 1955) and Robert M. MacIver, *Academic Freedom in our Time* (New York: Columbia University Press, 1955).

courage to envisage new methods of inquiry and new ways of organizing research. In a deep sense, human truth must ever be willing to destroy itself in order to remain true to its very purpose. Every decent scholar must hope that his disciples may prove him wrong; to be a link in the chain that points toward the infinite is his spur and satisfaction.

Thus, when we ask for the causes of the change from the university of the Middle Ages to the scientific modern university, we may discover what looks like a sequence of acts of disloyalty to old and venerated values. Conservatives have often explained it this way. But underneath there is a dynamic, though often tortuous loyalty, the loyalty to the ideal of truth, which, like a diamond, shows ever changing facets to the human eye. In comparison with this long and persistent current of loyalty, the effects of social, political, and ecclesiastical pressures appear but as minor waves in the great river of human rationality.

Another comforting thought emerges when we look at the history of universities in perspective. In spite of all the changes from one period of rational self-consciousness to the other, no movement of ideas that has been profound and helpful to men in their endeavor to explain themselves and their relation to the universe has ever entirely disappeared. Aristotle is no longer "the teacher," as he was for Thomas Aquinas. Paris is no longer the old scholastic university; if it were it would be a negligible institution. The humanist and Protestant universities have changed their character; some of them, like Erfurt and Herborn, have even ceased to exist. Everywhere the law of change seems to have prevailed over man's desire for continuity. Yet Aristotelian scholasticism, or Thomism, is still on the field, and so is humanism and the Protestant concept of religion. The enlightened *philosophes* of the eighteenth century are still admired, and no empirical science, positivism, or existentialism, however important, will ever make negligible the questions and answers proposed by the idealist systems. The orchestration becomes more varied, sometimes even confused and confusing, but the leading themes or *leitmotifs* remain. That which has at any time made it deeper and richer, the human soul is unlikely to forget. It is not so ungrateful as it seems to be. And now, with our intellectual life becoming increasingly international, the old wisdom of Asia has also begun to attract the interest and even the commitment of the curious student. When, as is natural in the context of this essay, we look especially at American higher education, we find every great movement represented. Aristotelian Thomism, for example, is still taught in our Catholic universities. This variety of movements and institutions may partly be due to the fact that the United States is a country of immigrants from many parts of the world, who bring with them the lore of their homelands. But it has its reason also in the curiosity and vitality of the American mind.

An additional factor, however, makes for a certain instability in American academic life. We have already alluded to it. In contrast with other countries, though with a certain resemblance to the English system, American higher education is divided into the preprofessional, or liberal undergraduate college, and the professional graduate schools. And though the teachers in the first are required to enrich their teaching by research, and though in our big universities the best scholars often teach on both the graduate and the undergraduate levels, the American college is not merely a scholarly, it is also an educational, institution. This is all the more true as a result of the democratic character of American society and the particular role of the high school, which means that the American college harbors many more students than institutions of higher education in any other country. More than three million students are taught by more than 250,000 teachers in the almost two thousand institutions on the post-high-school level. And the predictions are that by about

1960 the number will increase to 4,600,000 students, including 2,500,000 in the first two years, 1,500,000 in the last two years, and 600,000 graduate students.

It is the educational obligation of American colleges, over and above their scholarly functions, that provides the reason for the bewildering changes in their programs since the turn of the eighteenth century. Here lies also the explanation for the growth and complexity of the mechanisms of administration, and the modification of admission and graduation requirements, and of all the tutoring, guidance, and test procedures, which remind the foreign visitor sometimes more of his secondary school years than of his university studies.

V

But there is a still more fundamental source of the restless perpetuity and perpetual restlessness of Western higher education, and of Western education in general, and that is a particular conception of the nature of man. Every developed civilization, of course, has some such conception. The Western conception is a unique combination of Greek and Christian traditions with all their mutual tensions and complementations. This concept of man and of human society has assumed different forms in different countries. I am convinced, however, that, after much struggle and sacrifice, it has found its most comprehensive cultural expression in the kind of human organization associated with the idea of democracy. By no means is this to say that this idea has ever been realized perfectly or that the so-called American way of life is the only path to social fulfillment. In part, certain values appropriate to democracy may be achieved by measures alien to the American mind.

But whatever qualifications we may wish to add, the concept of man suggested here is based on the belief that every individual, irrespective of birth, class, and wealth, has the right and duty to develop the humanly desirable potentialities in his personality as fully as possible, to strive for truth and to reject untruth, to assert the demands of his conscience, even against the power of earthly and ecclesiastical governments, and to achieve under sympathetic guidance an ever-deepening understanding of himself, his relation to his fellow men, and to the great universe of which he is a part. That is what we understand by the freedom and dignity of man, or what is meant when the American Declaration of Independence speaks of the "inalienable rights of man." Without these prerequisites there can be no real justice, no real love, and no real progress.

Though this concept of man is individualistic, it is not asocial. On the contrary, it assumes that a good society and individual freedom, disciplined through the recognition of the highest values of humanity, condition and reinforce each other. Nor is this concept in any way opposed to the scientific understanding of nature and the human being. However deterministic and causal the methods of science may be, the greater man's knowledge, the greater will also be his capacity to live in accordance with the productive laws of existence. For freedom is not opposed to the recognition of one's belonging; it is the way of knowing where one belongs.

Yet today no thinking man can look without apprehension at certain collectivistic concepts and organizations of society which claim to be scientific or rational and even do provide a desirable degree of physical welfare, but have no respect for the "inalienable rights of man." They may even spread knowledge, but the knowledge is controlled and regulated, often even misleading. No country is free from this danger, for the complexity of our political and economic situation encourages—and perhaps even demands—an ever-increasing amount of concentration of power and control. Nor can one free himself from fear of certain developments in science which, if used for humane purposes, could lead mankind to unimagined heights, but might otherwise push it into a new form of serfdom and misery.

It has been said with good reason that victory in the strife of nations will fall to the group able to produce the largest and most efficient instruments of construction—and of destruction. And there can be no doubt that the institutions of higher education are the indispensable instruments for developing this power. Our colleges and universities would fail to do their duty if they did not help their nations and, so they hope, all mankind to be strong scientifically. And wherever one looks, more and more of the intellectually gifted youth see their personal fulfillment in scientific work.

But does that perhaps mean that advanced education all over the world will offer itself as usher to an era of highly organized and scientific form of neobarbarism, destroying the results of man's painful self-liberation? And may the increasing number of students who will populate the universities—in the United States already reaching into the millions—bring about the highly perilous combination of two seemingly contradictory factors— high intellectual development on one side and impoverishment of character on the other? Academic man is inclined to over- estimate the theoretical component of civilization, forgetting that a mature man needs an intellect balanced by an equally serious cultivation of his emotional and active qualities. It takes a well- bred scholar to realize the limitations and dangers of one-sided scholarship. When, then, more and more young people leave the lecture rooms and laboratories, many of them with the feeling that they have arrived at the pinnacle of human achievements after they have passed their examinations, and when more and more instructors must be hired merely because they somehow master their subject matter without realizing their deeper ob- ligations as educators of youth, will this perhaps produce a society top-heavy with specialized intellectual efficiency, but indifferent to the subtle values which guarantee the depth, the charm, and the harmonious progress of human life? Here lies the enormous responsibility of a truly liberal and preprofessional education. Whether, as in some countries, it is mainly relegated to selective secondary schools, or whether, as in the United States, it is the task of undergraduate colleges, it remains an essential obligation. Nor can even the specialized professional studies free themselves from the obligation to produce not only "experts," but men who see their specialties in the wider context of human interests and who wish to apply their expertise to the good of mankind.

The history of higher education shows that its institutions have alienated themselves from the spirit of their period, or have decayed into glorified trade schools, whenever they have not seen the necessity of a productive interaction between scholarship and human culture. Only when they have been able to combine the advancement of knowledge with the interpretation and guardianship of the deeper meanings of human existence have they been really respected.[11] This synthesis is today more difficult than

[11] Robert Ulich, "On the Rise and Decline of Higher Education," in *Goals for American Education*, ed. L. Bryson, L. Finkelstein, R. M. MacIver. Ninth Symposium on the Conference on Science, Philosophy, and Religion (New York: Harper and Brothers, 1950).

We possess no work that covers the whole history of Western higher education. A highly valuable, though not always satisfactory attempt has been made by Stephen d'Irsay in his *Histoire des universités françaises et etrangères des origines à nos jours*, 1936. The best account of the medieval university in English is to be found in Hastings Rashdall, *The Universities of Europe in the Middle Ages*. New edition by F. M. Powicke and A. B. Emden. (Oxford: Clarendon Press, 1936).

There exist monographs about almost all the greater universities of the western world. For literature on higher education in the United States see the following works, most of which have extensive bibliographies: John S. Brubacher and Willis Rudy, *Higher Education in Transition. A History of American Colleges and Universities, 1636–1956* (New York: Harper and Brothers, 1958). R. Freeman Butts, *The College Charts its Course. Historical Conceptions and Current Proposals* (New York: McGraw-Hill Book Company, Inc., 1939).

ever. But one may confidently hope that, despite the disappointing narrowness and complacency of many teachers, our colleges and universities are aware of the challenge offered to them in one of the greatest periods of transition in human history.

Goals for American Education, ed. L. Bryson, L. Finkelstein, R. M. MacIver. Ninth Symposium on the Conference on Science, Philosophy and Religion (New York: Harper and Brothers, 1950). George P. Schmidt, *The Liberal Arts College. A Chapter in American Cultural History* (New Brunswick: Rutgers University Press, 1957). Richard J. Storr, *The Beginnings of Graduate Education in America* (Chicago: University of Chicago Press, 1953).

3.

Science and the

Human Community

J. ROBERT OPPENHEIMER
Director, The Institute for Advanced Study

My main function in this chapter must be to initiate a conversation among us. The question I wish to discuss is that of the effects of the development of science on the nature of our culture, and, therefore, on its educational problems. One could take a comparative approach to this question, either in space or in time. One could take the institutions and the science of the United States, for example, and compare them with England's, or Japan's, or Turkey's. Or one could make the comparison temporal, asking, as is the habit, "Why are things so much more difficult? Why is everything so much worse than it was?" I do not, however, propose to do either of these things. In particular, I have a nervous feeling about most of our educational and cultural comparisons with the past.

It is true that in the eighteenth and nineteenth centuries in England there was a form of limited liberal education which had, both at the time and in retrospect, great charm and coherence. But it was not, in my opinion, really serious higher education at all. Its purpose was the molding of a common sensibility and a common coherence in a small group of men destined to play a big part in the history of their country, and indeed in the history of the world. For its purpose it was valuable. But I do not think that anyone today can seriously suppose that reading Horace and even learning him by heart is a unique or necessary condition for being a learned man or for being an educated man.

48

The problem faced by this older style in education was different from any that we face, if only because of the small number of people involved. And it was different, too, in its intense, cultivated effort at provincialism. This effort is almost the opposite of the effort that we think we must make today, when we would very much like to have people learn the differences between cultures—knowing all the time, of course, that if this is to be useful knowledge, they still must also have a true culture of their own.

I also know, of my own direct observation, that in most fields of learning the education which is available in an American university today is incontestably superior to that which was available when I was a young man in college thirty years ago. The comparison in physics is almost as night and day; and I have little doubt that what I say is true of other fields of natural science, though I cannot speak with the same direct knowledge. There are exceptions. I would say that a man thirty years ago could learn perhaps more warmly, and with a greater interest, the early stages of the study of philosophy than may be possible today. At my school, at any rate, I think I was lucky to be studying philosophy in the twenties and not in the fifties. But in almost all subjects, it is the other way around. I am not saying that the young people of today get a better education. This is a vast subject which we shall never finish discussing. But I am saying that their teachers know more, and teach more, and on the whole, I think, teach better. The variety is greater, the expertise and mastery are greater, the civility is greater, and the civilization is greater.

Nevertheless, I do have the impression that what thirty years ago in this country hardly appeared as a revolutionary and wholly novel problem, and what in some parts of the world may today hardly appear quite in those terms, has by now caught us up in a situation unparalleled in human history. It confronts us with difficulties which are not easy to resolve by turning to the past, though, in truth, they cannot be resolved by forgetting it; and it calls, above all, for a new definition of, and a new attitude toward, culture and toward communication, education, and learning. It is the attitude of accepting with a glad heart something of which men have for millenia spoken, and to which they have looked with a kind of horror. I have the impression that we are very much caught up in this situation in the United States, that it is going to grow, and that nothing—at any rate, nothing desirable—can stop it. I have the impression too that in Europe the problems that I am here going to outline are somewhat less articulated and somewhat less pressing, but that they are latent and are part of Europe's trouble, as they are of ours. I have the same impression of Japan, though I speak with an ignorance that grows as I get farther away from Princeton, New Jersey. And I have the further impression that the problems we are grappling with—cognitive and cultural problems—are destined to become world-wide, unless quite tragic things take place to prevent this.

One aspect of the problem about which I have been talking is suggested by a characteristic of contemporary American education to which I have already alluded. It is something which probably overwhelms many visitors to American universities. This is the increasing number of people who go on to increasingly later stages—and, one may hope, higher levels—of education. This is surely a process which is under way in other countries, though it is in very different stages in various parts of the world and is probably more advanced in the United States than elsewhere. The proportion of people who spend their time up to, let us say, their twenty-first or twenty-fourth year in primarily educational pursuits is probably larger in this country than anywhere else. But events are clearly moving in a similar direction throughout the world.

But although this is a serious element in the general problem, it is not the heart of the matter; for quite apart from the sheer matter of numbers, the educational and cultural problem is vaster than it has ever been before. The underlying economy today, along with the more extended educational opportunities that are available, promises very, very much leisure in man's life, very much opportunity for cultivation of the mind, very much opportunity for reading, for playing music, for painting, for drama, for the dance, and for learning. It is already a different world from what it was a hundred years ago. This, again, I think is more acute in the United States; but surely it is our desire that this development—or this problem, if we wish to formulate it as a problem—be a universal one. Surely, only things that we would universally deplore would prevent its becoming universal. And this development is accompanied by something else which also seems to me undesirable to try to reverse. There is a kind of unheirarchical character to our society, something noted long ago by all thoughtful visitors, especially by de Tocqueville, a willingness to leave to the voluntary hands of a large population the ordering and organization of people, of interests.

You see it in our cultures. I am sure that wherever the visitor to America goes, he finds voluntary groups that put on plays better, I think, in most ways than what he could see on Broadway, and voluntary groups that play music, and voluntary groups that talk about problems of science, and problems of politics. This enormous unorganized and uninstitutionalized and totally nonhierarchical sort of activity is typical of the United States. But I do not think it is something which the older, more ordered societies of Europe and Asia will long be without. Americans, in any case, are deeply dedicated to it, and an American society, ordered from the top and ordered uniquely, ordered monolithically, in which everybody knew who was the best scientist, who was the best composer, which was the best band, would be a repugnant one. In fact, the attempt by the magazines, by the press, by the television outfits, to create such an order is resisted by the strongest tool of the American public, which is their laughter. They know that these ratings are transitory, and they pay very little attention to them.

There is another side to the story, however, and it is perhaps best put brutally. In the seventeenth century the sense of a new world began to spread, and the feeling that the old order had been shot out from under was sharply articulated. Some of the finest poetry of our history was written as a result. And people also began to talk about a possibility which, in the eighteenth century, especially in France and England, was referred to with awe and apprehension. A time might not be far off, it was suggested, when the sum of human knowledge would double every half century. It is arguable whether the doubling time of knowledge today is eight years or eleven years; but it is something like that. And this extraordinary acceleration has been achieved by the development in the full, broad, noble sense of the word *science*. It is most strikingly true in the natural sciences and can even be measured by volume of publication. And this increase in quantity does not signify by any means that quality has declined. A society will protect itself from really trivial things: a group of physicists or a group of biochemists will manage their journals in such a way that what is in those journals is worth reading to the specialist. The quality, I would say, in all branches of science in which I have either knowledge or competence or interest has gone up with the fantastic increase in quantity.

Now this knowledge is, of course, not without its order. In fact, it is all about order. It whole purpose is to relate experiences to each other and to show that not everything in human experience is arbitrary. But it is not orderly in the sense that there are a few general premises from which you can deduce everything else. And it never will be. The conviction which the physicist may have that the facts of chemistry could be deduced from physics if someone tried doesn't mean that chemistry is a part of physics. And it should not be at all. The interesting parts of chemistry are those which no physicist would ever have thought of deducing. Similarly, we may be confident about the great insights into the origin of life, and the nature of genetic material, and the coding techniques which all living organisms have and which dominate such primitive things as perception. We may be confident that there will be a total lack of gap between the biological and psychological descriptions of man. Still, this will never reduce the parts of psychology to biology.

This enormous house of science has its inner relatedness, which is very subtle and beautiful, but it is not the sort of edifice that was imagined in the enlightenment of a century ago. What we have is entirely different from the early nineteenth-century nightmare of Laplace, who thought that one had only in a static moment to be temporarily omniscient and all history could be predicted out of this moment of insight. What we have today corresponds to an entirely different ideal of human knowledge, in which from the very beginning it is understood that if you pursue one means of sorting out our experience, you exclude many or all others. From the very beginning, starting with the most elementary, common-sense things, scientific activity today marches off in different technical and specialized directions and adopts and cultivates a view of knowledge as something which, in its nature, cannot be total, but is always partial and self-limited.

Now all this means that the problem of acculturation, and the problem of community, and the problem of education—they are all related problems—have a character for us which is quite different from any they have had in the past. I have often been led to recall with interest a metaphor which William James used fifty years ago to describe the nature of the interrelations in our cognitive world. He saw this world not as global, not as made up of the kind of description which one would give of a finite, closed object, like a temple, which was there for all time and which one might survey and describe and come back to again and again until no further detail needed to be added. He saw it rather as an affair of networks or interconnections of relevance, some explicit, some remote: an affair in part of analogies, some recognized and some not recognized, perhaps formal analogies of the kind that mathematics uses so much, perhaps logical analogies, perhaps often analogies that are verbal and rather thin, and sometimes even the affective analogies which play so enormous a part in the arts. It is a set of interconnections, not themselves exhaustible, between rapidly growing, highly specialized, and enormously fruitful ways of knowing about the world. And the problem of domesticating this intricate and novel system of beliefs and procedures in the more general culture around us has, therefore, certain distinctive and troublesome features.

Before proceeding, there are two points I should like to add which may make matters a little sharper. The first has to do with our knowledge of man. I believe there is a good chance that what have been the protosciences of man are now rather close to becoming the many, many different sciences of man. I do not think that in the world fifty years from now there will be a subject called *psychology*, any more than there is now a subject called *natural philosophy*. I think that different ways of studying man will lead to disciplines which for convenience will have different names, be in different buildings, and will have different professors. But I believe that we are on the threshold of an enormous enrichment in what we know about man. I do not mean that we will ever know more, in a certain sense, than we can find from the greatest art. But that is something very different. It is something that we rightly cherish, and it must be evident that I am not trying to exclude it from the sum of human life. But it is not the kind of knowledge I am talking about. I have in mind rather the same sort of homely, and in the end sometimes forbiddingly dull, knowledge that we get to have about such magic things as the stars and about life itself. In fact, we never answer the questions which people thought would be answered when they asked, "Will we ever understand life?" or "Will we ever understand what makes the stars move in their courses?" We understand other things and we answer other questions. And so it will be with the sciences of man. But I do have the impression that all the way from history to biology a great arc of science is about to catch fire. We have to be prepared to deal with this and to see that it does not throw us off balance and does not even further corrupt and corrode the vitality of our society.

The second point about the growth of modern knowledge, which I should like to stress before proceeding to the broader cultural and educational problem, has to do with the nature of scientific communities. The receptacle of all the knowledge we have, the agencies to whom this knowledge is entrusted and who create it, are not individual men. They are communities of men. They are the specialized professions, often increasingly special- ized. The world of knowledge is a world held together by little bands of people who know a great deal about some particular field but whose relations with neighboring fields, while warm, are often not very intense. As far as the world of learning goes, we live in a way in a kind of generalization of the old medieval guilds, a kind of syndicalism which is a cognitive syndicalism, a syndicalism in which the true community, the true intimate col- laboration of men, is best exemplified by groups of specialists who understand each other and help each other. Every scholar is in some sense or other a member of such a group. To use the image of a network again, these communities offer a picture of internal intimacy, cognitive intimacy, an intimacy of understanding and clarity, and usually also of good will and cordiality; and these communities stretch through all parts of the world. One notices this fact with hope, but one notices it also with melancholy. For one thinks of these communities as networks holding the world together, and one cannot believe that these bonds are strong enough for the times we live in.

But now we must come to the relation of this knowledge and these communities to the larger world in which they have emerged and which they affect. There are two traits of this world that I would stress, two things which seem to me to mark it off from past times—certainly from the Athens that we love, certainly from the high times in Elizabethan England, or the Enlightenment, or the great days of the Renaissance: all of them times of change, of great discovery, of unmooring. The first thing I would single out about the present scene is the overwhelming predominance of things that are new over things that are old. This is, of course, a consequence of the fact that knowledge doubles every ten years. It expresses itself in the fact that no professional man can really be any good if he does not, either by formal schooling or by reading and his own efforts, really keep at school constantly. No engineer can leave school today and hope to be a competent engineer in relation to the problems of twenty years from now if he has not gone back to school or done the equivalent. And this phenomenon shows itself, of course, not only in matters of sheer knowledge. The application of knowledge changes the face of the earth. It is brilliantly illustrated in towns like São Paulo in Brazil, which simply grew as you watched. It has been very much illustrated on the face of Europe, and it is of course illustrated in the United States. People do not live as they did even ten, twenty, or thirty years ago. The kinds of practices their parents engaged in, the kind of sensibility their parents had, live on in a new and rather alien soil. This has come about partly from mechanical changes, partly from the changes brought about by communication, partly from the actual change in what people know. And this imbalance between the new and the old, although it is not beyond endurance for man, is something to which man is unaccustomed and for which his tradition has not fully prepared him.

The second trait of the present scene which I would stress is another kind of imbalance. If we look at what is known, the proportion that is known by specialized groups is very large, and the proportion that gets back into the common knowledge of man is very small. I have a prejudice—perhaps some Englishman will correct me—that England has done best in putting special knowledge into the common pool of knowledge of educated men. It is not put in very deeply; it is not put in with terribly much reverence. But that is the price you pay for putting it in at all. And this is almost not done at all in the United States. As a result, there is a deep attrition of the common culture. The common culture does not receive the kind of resources which it should be getting from the special expeditionary forces that are going off in all directions and learning so many new things. These expeditions do not enrich the common culture because almost no solid report comes back from them. The transmittal back is entrusted too much to woefully superficial and often meretricious popularizations, which do not get the meaning, or the beauty, or the weight of the experience communicated, and which do not, in a certain sense, engage or involve the general public. Even within a large part of science itself, I know that one specialist does not get a feeling for what goes on in a contiguous specialty. As I have been forced to note with amazement, there is today practically no understanding among physicists, for example, of what modern mathematicians are doing. There is a good deal of, perhaps not boredom, but suspicion that mathematicians are engaged in a game that will

never be a part of the physicists' world. And I am afraid the
mathematicians hold the same attitude in reverse and think the
physicists are bothering about rather foolish things, which, if
only they could really be cleared up, the mathematician would
understand very clearly. But the mathematician is not going to
turn his mind to such problems for a long, long time.

We have, then, a predominance of novelty on the present
scene, and also an absence of common knowledge, or at least
a thinning of common knowledge, together with an enormous
growth of specialized and available knowledge, but not vital,
living knowledge. And both these tendencies give one the sense
that what in the past people have called *values* are bound to
suffer. For whatever values may be, they rest in areas of life
which are familiar and deeply intimate. Though one can think
of exceptions, they have for the most part a dual character. On
the one hand, they are commitments, commitments as to where
one stands, and where one acts, and what one will be, and what
one cares for. On the other hand, they always involve memories.
Thus, in values, commitment and memory unite the past and the
future. And so, with the enormously rapid change in our lives,
partly cognitive, partly technical and practical, it is not unnatural
that we should have a sense of evaporation and emasculation and
vagueness in this area. Our past is not so manifestly meaningful
for our future. The problems that we meet in our future are not
like those which we suffered and from which we learned in our
youth, even though there are some analogies. And the danger is
that if people today articulate what they think about the good
and the beautiful, their words will have a kind of awesome
vagueness, an awesome lack of the specific and the robust and
the intimate. The business of human life, after all, has to be the
business of using what we were to become what we shall be. And
this means that just the things that you have been close to, that
you have felt as well as learned, that you have learned to do

and learned about, that you have learned as arts, things that you have been with for a while and have not changed too rapidly —these must still be present, and they must be relevant to you, to your colleagues, your associates, your community, your society, and your future.

But if human values are so much a matter of familiarity and intimacy, one might reply, "Why can't all this rapid change be stopped?" But it is obvious that such a change can be stopped only by two kinds of thing. There was a great Moslem renaissance, for example, which lasted over three centuries, but which stopped about the year 1100. And what stopped it can take place again. It was military conquest and religious orthodoxy. But without some horrible combination of these two devices, it is clear that men's curiosity, their adventuresomeness, even their cupidity, will all conspire to favor the conditions for the wonderful growth of knowledge with which we live. There are countries where the pace of change is something which people would have liked to resist, countries where many people would prefer not to let things like mechanization and large-scale industrialization go very fast. But in our world this course is not open; it is not a real possibility, short of a total calamity or a total tyranny. I think that it is our mission—if we have any influence—to avoid such an apocalypse and to avert the kind of fanatic ordering of belief and knowledge and activity which could put some fixity back into our cultural and practical lives. I think that we have to accept the situation that I have outlined.

But if we do, then, above all, we have to recognize that the notions of education and the notions of culture which we have inherited, and which were natural a century ago and still more natural several centuries ago, are today misleading and quite sure to lead us to do the wrong things. And while we recognize this, it must bring us to cherish the thing which is so in danger in the world. This is just the touch of intimacy, of craftsmanship, of skill, of true, deep understanding, ranging all the way from simple things in human life to the most recondite things that one can learn in mathematics or biology or history: love of the expert, love of style, love of technical competence. We have to do this at the same time that we know that whatever little we happen to have that is familiar and intimate is only one of an incredible number of things, most of which are rather remote from us. We learn about them through friends, through reading, by luck. We shall not learn them unless we are very fortunate—and very talented. There is a balance we must strike: on one side there must be a kind of openness and skepticism, a welcoming of the new and the unfamiliar; on the other side, there must be a passionate devotion and appreciation of intellectual excellence among all excellencies, of intimacy among all intimacies.

This view has implications for higher education. I shall not labor all of them. But one basic implication is that no man should escape our universities without knowing how little he knows. He must have some sense of the fact that not through his fault, not through his sloth (though he may be lazy and not very bright) but inherently in the nature of things, he is going to be an ignorant man and so is everyone else. It would be nice, however, if this great achievement could be complemented by another great achievement, which is to make a man, although he may be ignorant of almost everything, not quite ignorant of everything. My own feeling is that for education it is indeed necessary that it accomplish these two purposes. If I had to advise a young man, to give him some rule to live by, I know that the rule would be wrong most of the time and that my advice would only be safe if it were ignored. But if I did have to give such advice, I would be inclined to say, "Try to learn something very well indeed. And do not just learn what it is in general terms. Learn it as a practitioner; learn how to do it. And stop while you are doing it long enough to see the beauty of it." But I would not quite stop with that. I would add, "But learn something else as well that is quite different. Get some sense of the span of things human, the span of things that the intelligent man can cope with."

At least as far as science is concerned, I think I would trust such an approach far more than what has come to be called "the general-education approach," and which is essentially a description—essentially a journalistic description, though it may be very good journalism—of what has gone on in broad areas of science. I know that one has to have some sense of the connection of things, and that if the network of our culture is many dimensional and infinitely complex, one needs at least a few projections of this network on planes that can be looked at. Survey courses and general accounts of things serve a necessary purpose only because without them one cannot navigate. One has to learn how to use a dictionary; one also needs to know what ichthyology is. But I do not think that this is education; it is only a kind of general preparation of people for navigating about in the network.

I believe that the young people in the United States—and there are others, including many visitors to our universities, who know more about this than I do—are in a mood in which the kind of educational experience I have described would not be entirely unfamiliar and would not seem entirely foolish to them. Compared to any times I have known, the young people in this country seem less optimistic, less confident of the future. They do not really hope that there will be pie in the sky by and by. And since they look less to the future as the time of happiness and reward, they are very much less Puritan, and, in an important sense, very much less Protestant. They are in an almost equally important sense, therefore, somewhat more medieval. To find this in the middle of the turmoil of the twentieth century is rather odd. But it is also, I believe, a form of protection. The reason why there is more music and art on the campuses of the United States than ever before is partly because people are living for the moment. It is also partly because they have lost confidence to some extent in the ability of society automatically to reward the diligent. And it is also partly because in a kind of external conformity, an enormous internal freedom and spontaneity is often born.

There is one final thing that I would add. The communities that make, cherish, and foster knowledge and the arts are international communities. And in this age, even if we cannot see clearly what to do about it, we can see clearly that the sovereign, unlimited, all-powerful nation-state is a pretty deadly and impossible form for the organization of mankind. One should look with peculiar hopefulness, therefore, to the innocent international communities which, either in the gathering of knowledge or in its application, do bind people together from all over the world. That is, indeed, what so many physicists throughout the world have been shouting for the last twelve years or so. It has usually been a rather muted shout, as in the case of Niels Bohr, but it has been a very deep and heartfelt shout. This hope is what animated some of the first efforts in the United States after the war to suggest ways of coping with the new problems of atomic energy. The creation of vital, strong, international communities must precede the creation of international organs of comparable strength and vitality. And this, in turn, is probably what must precede the formal regulation of the sovereign national will. This national will even today, is, in fact, subject to constraints which as little as thirty years ago would have been regarded as unthinkable.

4.

The Democratization
of Educational Opportunity

JOHN HOPE FRANKLIN
Professor of History
Brooklyn College

The movement to broaden educational opportunities is a significant part of the American experience. It has been as important for higher education as it has been for education at the lower levels. In the colonial period, long before there was any notion that there was a public responsibility for education, the settlers embraced the view that some opportunities for higher education should exist on the Western side of the Atlantic, if only to prevent those who "hungered for the mysteries of learning" from being compelled to return to Europe as an alternative to being deprived of an education altogether. To be sure, there was no thought of extending these opportunities to more than the few, primarily those few who were preparing for the ministry. As one college after another opened its doors in the seventeenth and eighteenth centuries, however, there was a trend, even in this undertaking, toward extending opportunities to a larger number.

Nevertheless, as long as the view prevailed that the main function of higher education was to provide a trained ministry for the colonies, there was no general disposition to extend it to any considerable number of people or to people with a wide variety of intellectual interests. There persisted, moreover, the view that there was little relationship between delving into the mysteries of science and language on the one hand and clearing the wilderness and achieving a degree of material affluence on the other. But with the winning of independence and the broadening of the base of participation in public affairs, education gained in importance, and the notion of public responsibility for higher education achieved some ascendancy and respectability. The Delaware journalist and teacher, Robert Coram, spoke for an increasing number of Americans when he said in 1791 that every citizen "has an equal right to subsistence, and ought to have an equal opportunity of acquiring knowledge." Some states—Georgia and North Carolina, for example—took the first wavering steps toward establishing public universities; and at the seat of the federal government there was much talk of setting up a national university.

Within a half century after independence the tide favoring the broadening of educational opportunities was beginning to rise. The most important single factor in this development was the strong conviction of the newly enfranchised citizens of the Jacksonian period and later that education was indispensable to their effective participation in government. "Can freedom long dwell where ignorance and vice prevail?" asked Caleb Atwater in 1841. He was convinced that it could not; and he called on the American people to "lay a foundation broad, deep, and high, building on it the means of instruction, which shall eventually, like a crucible, melt down the whole mass of our citizens into one lump of liquid, living, active, moving virtue and intelligence." Education was, therefore, not only to prepare citizens to function in a democracy, but it was to foster and preserve the very spirit of democracy and create in America "a nation of brothers."

State governments as well as religious and philanthropic agencies apparently took the cue from Atwater and his compatriots. In the middle years states such as Massachusetts and Illinois that had not established public colleges and universities proceeded to do so. As new states like Wisconsin and Minnesota came into the Union, they early committed themselves to programs of public higher education. Practically every major religious denomination founded colleges and universities as important parts of their effort to win and hold persons committed to their particular faith. Northwestern University, Notre Dame, and the University of the South are cases in point. The secular influence was also at work; and persons who favored private education free of religious influences established nonsectarian colleges and universities such as Beloit, Union, and Rochester. The philanthropists who made great fortunes during and after the Civil War were also to share in the program of democratizing educational opportunities by founding institutions like Cornell, Vanderbilt, and Stanford.

In the middle years, from 1830 to 1870, the broadening of educational opportunities had a particularly salutary effect on the status of two groups—women and Negroes—that hitherto had been regarded as outside the pale. As early as 1819 Emma Willard had insisted that women should be educated to be the "companions not the satellites of men." When Oberlin College opened its doors in 1833 it embraced the views of Emma Willard and accepted women on the same basis as men. Meanwhile, white Americans had discussed the intellectual capabilities of the Negro since the time that Jefferson had taken up the subject in his correspondence with the Abbé Grégoire, the French scholar, and Benjamin Banneker, the Negro mathematician. They had reached no definitive conclusions, and not until the founding of Oberlin College, which accepted Negroes as students, did black men begin to enjoy the opportunity to obtain a college education in the United States.

Before the end of the nineteenth century the problem of higher education for women had virtually been solved. Public colleges and universities were recognizing their obligation to educate women and were gradually accepting them on a basis of equality with men. Even the new programs of vocational and agricultural education, financed by federal funds under the Land Grant Act, took cognizance of the importance of educating women. The philanthropists also did their part in providing new opportunities for the education of women by founding such colleges as Vassar, Smith, and Bryn Mawr. Democratic higher education in the United States had made significant strides by 1900.

The impression should not be conveyed, however, that there was universal acceptance of the principle of democracy in higher education or of the assumptions underlying it. Some Americans persisted in their belief that universal education was not necessarily beneficial even to those who received it. As late as 1890 the Governor of Virginia declared that he regarded education as a luxury exclusively for those who could afford it; and in several states there was strong sentiment against taxation for the support of higher education. The democratization of educational opportunity was most vigorously resisted whenever it applied to Negroes, and it was in this area that the final battles were to be fought.

The obstacles in the way of extending full opportunities in the area of higher education to Negroes were both numerous and formidable. In the nineteenth century the contention that the Negro was mentally incapable of securing an advanced education was widespread in the United States and especially in the Southern states, where more than 90 per cent of the Negroes lived. The Negro's mental inferiority had been one of the arguments advanced in defense of slavery, and it did not disappear with emancipation. Southerners "generally laugh at the idea of the Negro learning," declared J. D. B. De Bow in 1866; and this was because the whites had become "accustomed to the idea that Negroes are pretty stupid." Even if they did have the capacity to learn, any training beyond the mere rudiments was regarded as socially unsound. Some commentators argued, furthermore, that higher education for Negroes would be disastrous, because from it Negroes would inevitably get "false and foolish notions of equality" that would make them unsuited for the servile roles they were destined to play. Finally, since higher education was very expensive, particularly for the South with its very limited resources, and since any provisions for higher education in the South were therefore made begrudgingly, there was the general feeling that education for Negroes should be the first thing sacrificed when it was necessary to curtail expenditures for education.

Thus, in the years immediately following the Civil War, when Southern governments were in the hands of former leaders of the Confederacy, no provision whatever was made for public higher education of Negroes. Indeed, almost nothing was done for the public education of Negroes at any level. The schools and colleges open to Negroes were founded and supported by the Freedmen's Bureau and by religious and philanthropic agencies. When the so-called "Radicals" took over the Southern governments in 1868 they recognized the importance of universal public education and took steps to provide such education for blacks as well as whites. They even opened some of the formerly all-white colleges and universities to Negroes, but such moves were bitterly opposed by the whites who promptly withdrew their sons from such desegregated institutions. As the Southern whites recovered control of their state and local governments, they took pains to establish in law the principle of segregation in education at every level. Public Jim Crow colleges (segregated Negro colleges) sprang up in each of the Southern states; and the public officials, including educational administrators, made no attempt, in founding and maintaining these institutions, to adhere to the principle of "separate but equal" facilities that had been enunciated by the Supreme Court in 1896. Too many white Southerners, through the policies they pursued, seemed to agree with Mississippi's Senator J. K. Vardaman when he declared in 1897 that all the money spent on the education of the Negro was a "positive unkindness" to him. "It simply renders him unfit for the work which the white man has prescribed, and which he will be forced to perform."

The educational opportunities provided by the public Negro colleges and universities could hardly be described as steps toward democracy. These institutions represented not only racial segregation and discrimination in its most refined form, but by their very existence they represented a rejection of science and objective scholarship. For these challenged the assumptions on which such institutions were based. Appropriations for these institutions, furthermore, were always niggardly, and the pressures on the Negro administrators and teachers made freedom of teaching or learning virtually impossible. In short, such institutions represented, at best, some gesture in the direction of the *form* of democratizing educational opportunity, but it can hardly be argued that they were a contribution in *substance* toward the actual democratization of educational opportunity. It was a most remarkable achievement of these Jiw Crow colleges and universities that they did succeed in training, under extremely unfavorable conditions, a large number of men and women who became leaders in their respective fields. Meanwhile, in the white colleges and universities, the doctrine of white supremacy was all too frequently a regular part of the "intellectual armor" with which the student was equipped.

By the twentieth century the people of the United States were becoming increasingly committed to the proposition that the opportunity to secure a higher education was an important feature of a democratic society. The American people were not precise or clear in their understanding of the value of higher education, but they had come to the view that if the many were as entitled to primary and secondary education as the few they were similarly entitled to a chance at higher education. In taking this view, the American people were pursuing a course significantly different, in certain respects, from that pursued by most other countries. While Europeans were rigorously reexamining their systems of higher education and were beginning to open them to persons of ability regardless of social rank, the trend in the United States was to extend such opportunities much more rapidly, and to extend them, indeed, to all persons even when their ability was not clearly established. By comparison the task of the United States appeared simple. With its enormous resources it had merely to provide the opportunity for all; and those who availed themselves of the opportunity could prove their right to an education by their performance as students. Even if they failed from a strictly academic point of view, the opinion was that the nation had somehow gained from even this perfunctory exposure of its citizens to the higher learning. Not until much later in the twentieth century did America begin to doubt that it could provide a higher education for all who desired it. The bulging population, the mounting costs, and the shortage of teaching personnel were among the major considerations that created this new doubt.

But the task of the United States was made more complex by yet another consideration. Democratization of educational opportunity was not merely a matter of increasing available educational opportunity, even if the enormous resources of the country were adequate. It was also a matter of eliminating discrimination that tended to restrict the better opportunities to certain favored religious and racial groups. Thus, at the precise moment when unprecedented sums were being expended to increase higher educational opportunities, certain groups, such as Jews and Negroes, experienced difficulties in gaining admission to many colleges and universities. Tacit and overt quota systems for Jews in some graduate and professional schools and the systematic exclusion of Negroes from many were commonplace, and outright segregation of Negroes in the colleges and universities of the South was the rule. Beginning in the 1920s many institutions required applicants to supply data concerning their religion, the places of birth of their parents, and even the maiden name of their mothers. A special investigating committee of the New York City Council concluded in 1946 that the institutions were extremely anxious to "ascertain the racial origins, religion, and color of the various applicants for a purpose other than judging their qualifications for admission." This helps to explain the fact that, according to the Vocational Bureau of B'Nai B'rith, the proportion of Jewish students in 160 law schools dropped from 25.8 per cent in 1935 to 11.1 per cent in 1946, while the proportion in medical schools dropped from 16.1 per cent to 13.3 per cent for the same period.

These practices did not make a pretty picture as far as democracy in higher education was concerned. But the brand of bigotry spawned in Germany in the 1930s helped many Americans see not only the inhumanity of religious discrimination but the national stupidity of it as well. After World War II the United States not only proceeded to denazify Germany but to eliminate some practices of its own that discriminated against Jews. Colleges and universities began to renounce the principle of quotas for racial and religious groups. Some states threatened to withdraw tax-exempt privileges from institutions that practiced racial and religious discrimination. Some states forbade colleges and universities, even private ones, to require applicants for admission to answer questions about race or religion or to submit photographs with applications. Finally, the President's Commission on Higher Education in 1947 urged the nation to put an end to all undemocratic educational practices, such as racial and religious discrimination. By mid-century religious quotas were rapidly disappearing, and even the practice of keeping records on the basis of race or religion was becoming rare in university circles in the United States.

Yet there remained the most difficult problem of all in the matter of democratizing educational opportunity in the United States: that of bringing one-tenth of the nation's population, the Negro citizens, into the full enjoyment of the educational opportunities available to others in all parts of the country. The problem was deeply embedded in the history of the country, in its economy, its social order, its tragic Civil War, and its uneasy sectional peace. The quest for a solution had not always been made in good faith or with sufficient zeal. This was America's greatest failure in the field of education, and it was widely recognized as such by thoughtful men and women by the end of World War II. The failure was not merely that the educational programs available to Negroes were lamentably inadequate. The larger failure was the rejection of the basic principles that underlay the whole program of democratizing educational opportunity in the United States. Among these rejected principles was the view that an educated citizenry is one of democracy's greatest bulwarks and that equality of opportunity is fundamental to the successful functioning of a democracy.

None saw this with greater clarity than the President's Commission on Higher Education and none expressed more vigorously the importance of an early solution to the problem. The Commission recommended not only the elimination of inequalities in educational opportunities but the abandonment of all forms of segregation and discrimination in higher education. "Fundamental to this effort," the Commission contended, "must be a greatly increased will on the part of all citizens to see that justice is done. . . . There has been too much tardiness and timidity. It now seems clear that many institutions will change their policies only under legal compulsion." But it was clear that mere words, even when uttered by a group of such high standing as the President's Commission, were inadequate to cope with the difficult problem of breaking down racial barriers in education. For that task, as the Commission itself implied, vigorous, fearless action was needed; and it was provided primarily by the legal committee of the National Association for the Advancement of Colored People and by other groups and individuals sympathetic with such action.

Legal action to democratize educational opportunities for Negroes was necessitated by the intransigence of the Southern states on any and all questions related to the equality of Negroes before the law. The opposition to the exercise of the franchise by Negroes is a case in point. For more than thirty years Negroes sought to participate in the Democratic primary in the Southern states, and it was not until 1944 that a Supreme Court decision outlawed once and for all the exclusion of Negroes from the primary. The struggle to equalize the salaries of Negro and white teachers is another case in point. For a decade Southern school boards not only refused to grant Negro teachers equal pay for the same training and experience that white teachers had, but they usually terminated the services of Negro teachers who made such demands. The courts never gave school boards any comfort, however, and in every instance that such matters were litigated, Negro teachers were granted relief by the courts.

It was only natural, then, that under such circumstances legal action was required to democratize higher educational opportunities for Negroes. By 1930 the vast majority of Negroes who attended college were in exclusively or predominantly Negro institutions. They were, of course, scattered through many Northern institutions, but in small numbers. Meanwhile, the problem of graduate and professional training of Negroes increased as a larger number of Negroes sought kinds of training that was not provided by any public Negro colleges. Only a few private Negro colleges had any programs of graduate and professional education, while many Northern colleges either had racial quotas or were beyond the financial or geographical reach of most Negro aspirants. More and more, Negroes began to feel that Southern states should provide graduate and professional training for Negroes as well as whites. Several states, fearing the worst, began to provide out-of-state scholarships for Negro graduate and professional students.

Sending Negroes out of the state, however, was merely a temporary and unsatisfactory makeshift, as Southern states were soon to discover. In 1935 when a Negro sought admission to the law school of the University of Maryland, the state court of appeals made it clear that it regarded such scholarships for Negroes as unequal to the existing provisions for educating the whites and, therefore, a violation of the law. Three years later the United States Supreme Court declared that it was the duty of the state to provide education for *all* its citizens *within* the state if such education was provided for any of its citizens. This decision, perhaps more than any other, shocked and frightened the South into a realization that equal educational opportunity for all citizens was an expensive responsibility that was difficult to evade. Some states increased their out-of-state tuition; others established makeshift graduate and professional schools within the states. Chairs of law and overnight engineering schools for Negroes made their appearance in several Southern states.

In succeeding years the fight for graduate education within the Southern states continued. Negroes began to argue in the courts that the makeshift arrangement violated their rights. In Texas, Oklahoma, Kentucky, North Carolina, and elsewhere, they were challenging the segregated institutions, and the nation was entertained by the spectacle of distinguished professors, deans, and presidents of white state universities testifying under oath that the Negro institutions were equal in every respect to the older, well-established white universities. These contentions were brought to an abrupt and final disposition in 1950. In one case the Supreme Court declared that it was not possible for the Negro law school of Texas to provide the Negro student with an education equal to that of the university law school that had a strong faculty, experienced administrators, influential alumni, standing in the community, tradition, and prestige. In another case the court declared that when a Negro is admitted as a bona fide student to a university he cannot be subjected to any form of segregation or discrimination in the classroom, library, or cafeteria.

For most people, these were clear signs that the Supreme Court would, in time, open all public institutions of higher education to Negroes. A few, such as Arkansas, had admitted the first Negroes without litigation several years earlier. Others, such as the University of Louisville, merged with their Negro counterparts shortly after the 1950 decisions. After the 1954 decision outlawing segregation in the public schools, most of the Southern states regarded the decision as applicable to their public colleges. Within a few years a clear majority of the public colleges and universities in the Southern states were desegregated wholly or in part. By 1958 only four states, South Carolina, Georgia, Alabama, and Mississippi still had completely segregated systems of higher education.

There has been, of course, some considerable resistance to the clear trend toward the elimination of segregation in higher education. One form of resistance, rather innocent in appearance, has been the increased appropriations for Negro public colleges and graduate and professional schools in the hope that they-might be made so attractive that Negroes would not wish to enter the desegregated institutions. This is the kind of voluntary segregation in higher education that the governor of North Carolina has advocated for the public schools. Another form of resistance has been the rigging of admission requirements in such a way as to make it virtually impossible for a Negro to gain admission. If an applicant to a state university must submit supporting letters from the superintendent of schools (invariably white and therefore vulnerable to pressures) and several alumni living in the state (almost invariably segregationists) a Negro has little chance of meeting the requirements.

The most obvious and uncivilized form of resistance, however, has been the mob action to prevent matriculated Negro students from attending colleges and universities. In 1956, when the state of Alabama was ordered to admit a qualified Negro woman, the students and townspeople resorted to violence to prevent her from remaining at the University. When she was suspended because of the rioting, she accused university officials of conspiring to keep her out of the University. As a result the board of regents expelled her. Finally, there is the resistance of officials, usually state governors, who say simply and frankly that Negro applicants will not be admitted to the white state universities. Their position is so unequivocal that they take the view that any Negro who seeks admission to a white institution in opposition to their position is not sane. Thus, in the summer of 1958, when a Negro tried to gain admission to the University of Mississippi summer session, he was hustled off to an institution for the insane where he was placed under observation for several days. He was not declared to be of sound mind until he made it clear that he would make no further attempt to enter the University.

If the resistance to desegregation has been amazingly rigid in some instances, it can also be said that in some other instances acceptance of desegregation has been surprisingly prompt. Even before the significant court rulings affecting higher education, some public white colleges and universities had taken steps toward ending segregation. After the 1954 Supreme Court decision that outlawed segregation in public schools, many such institutions proceeded to desegregate without any significant manifestation of resistance or even resentment. Meanwhile, a considerable number of white private colleges and universities in the South, not directly affected by the Court decisions or other pressures, began to open their doors to qualified Negro applicants. In some cases they took the only steps toward desegregation to be taken in a community or state.

One interesting development that occurred in the wake of desegregation was the extension of new educational opportunities to prospective white students. When the colleges and universities of West Virginia and Missouri became desegregated, the former Negro state colleges discovered that many white students were not only willing but anxious to enroll. The favorable geographical locations of the colleges—in Jefferson City, Missouri, and near Charleston, West Virginia—opened educational opportunities to numerous white students that they had never known before. Consequently, white students enrolled by the hundreds and the former Negro colleges became fully desegregated almost overnight.

In the democratization of educational opportunity, the United States was sharing in an experience that seemed to be world-wide by the middle of the twentieth century. The impulse to push back the frontiers of knowledge and, at the same time, to democratize educational opportunity was quickening in many parts of the world. As the people of the world came to regard the right to know as something practically inalienable, they brought pressure to bear, in several different ways, on their leaders to place education within the reach of many, if not all. And as rivalries among the countries of the world became intensified, there was a notable acceleration of the drive to extend educational opportunities in order to use the available intellectual resources for national advancement. In such rivalry one could not always be certain that the extension of educational opportunity necessarily meant its democratization. In countries where extension of educational opportunity was to the politically orthodox students who were pledged to use their talents for the advancement of the interests of the state, the new opportunity could hardly be described as democratic. Yet, the pressures in such countries were real; and they resulted in the involvement of more people in the pursuit of higher education. The problem remained of how to make the new educational opportunities truly democratic and how to use them for the advancement of man rather than the state.

Even where democratization of educational opportunity proved a boon to society as well as to those who sought intellectual development, it created serious social and cultural problems, particularly in countries where traditional class lines tended to be rigid. In England, for example, the new provincial universities and the legislation of the 1940s brought new educational opportunities for the first time to large numbers. But new social and cultural tensions appeared as the sons of workingmen found themselves with the intellectual equipment that previously was the exclusive possession of gentlemen but without the social status and influence traditionally associated with that class. The task of assimilating the newly educated elements into the body politic and, at the same time, of utilizing them for the improvement of society was one of the most significant challenges that such communities and nations faced as they became committed to a new role for education in society.

Democratization of educational opportunity posed new educational problems that seemed to be inherent in the very development itself. As millions upon millions became involved in the pursuit of higher education, colleges and universities were compelled to adjust their organizational structure and intellectual fare to the needs of their constituents. They found it necessary to allow students greater freedom of choice in designing their educational careers in and out of the classroom. They had to continue the traditional functions of transmitting that which was known and of searching for new knowledge. They also had to take cognizance of the greater and greater variety of talents coming under their influence and to provide for the wide variety of occupational needs that were manifested. Finally, they had to find new ways in which the great masses of students could learn to function more effectively as members of a society that reflected the democracy for which the new higher education stood.

By 1958 the people of the United States were moving steadily toward the full democratization of educational opportunities. No longer were there any discriminations based on sex. Those based on religion were rapidly disappearing. Those based on race were under strong attack and were showing clear signs of receding to a point of less significance, if they were not disappearing altogether. These developments moved the American people significantly closer to a situation in which talent and, to some extent, financial ability were the only really crucial factors in the determination of who should obtain a higher education. (The increasing availability of public higher education at nominal expense has had the effect of mitigating the problem of financial ability.) As the nation moved toward the democratization of educational opportunity, it became possible, for the first time, for institutions of higher education to concern themselves with the process of education without any regard for the inhibiting factors of race, religion, and other irrelevancies. Thus the very atmosphere of learning was improved, indeed the air was cleared, as institutions, professors, and students began to devote themselves exclusively to the task of pursuing truth instead of defending or justifying spurious policies that were themselves a negation of the pursuit of truth.

Finally, this highly important development in the educational life of the nation represented a giant stride toward the solution of a major moral problem. In the task of reconciling American practice in human relations with the historic principles of democracy and equality to which the nation has been committed since its founding, it was desirable to enlist every available resource. With schools and colleges actively engaged in a program of becoming truly democratic, an important resource was becoming available for the task. In the process not only was the cry of hypocrisy becoming less shrill, but the moral position of the nation and its institutions was becoming more defensible. As the process continued, Americans in increasing numbers came to appreciate the importance of free and democratic educational institutions in the advancement of democracy in all other phases of life. Even before educational opportunities had become fully democratized, therefore, the salutary influence of such a process was being realized and appreciated. Perhaps this was sufficient to impel America to complete its task.

5.

The Responsibilities

and Freedoms of the Scholar

ROBERT B. BRODE
Professor of Physics
University of California

In our democratic society the scholar finds his natural home in the university. There he will find the greatest opportunity to fulfill his responsibilities and the fewest restrictions on his essential freedoms. There are endowed institutes, research foundations, hospitals, libraries, and government and industrial laboratories that support and encourage scholars. Some arbitrary and some necessary restrictions will, however, be found in these institutions that diminish the effectiveness of the scholar's efforts. A few institutes for advanced study and medical research foundations offer such unusual opportunities for research and study that they are, for some scholars, preferable to the academic institutions. But the majority of the scholarly profession choose the university for their place of work.

The young scholar is often motivated in his choice of a university position by the assurance of a comfortable livelihood together with the opportunity to continue the research program which absorbs his current interests. The more mature scholar chooses the university community because there he finds the greatest freedom to achieve his responsibilities. He also enjoys the congeniality and stimulation provided by his academic colleagues and by the students. He can expect little recognition from our society, perhaps, for his contributions to knowledge, but he will be appreciated and rewarded by his students and colleagues. The responsibilities of a scholar are not diminished by the impediments made by man or created by circumstances that frustrate him in his work. He may find that he cannot achieve his objectives because he is restricted by a lack of opportunity. While there must be a constant and continued effort to improve his opportunities, any limitation of his essential freedoms must be fought promptly and vigorously.

RESPONSIBILITIES

Wisdom, the first of the moral virtues, is indeed the first responsibility of the scholar. The totality of man's knowledge is a precious heritage that is entrusted to the scholar for preservation. In written form this knowledge is preserved in the libraries, seminars, and homes of the scholars. Lost arts, books, and skills are serious failures for our civilization and the discoveries of ancient documents, such as the Dead Sea Scrolls, are tremendous stimuli to students of ancient civilization. It is the responsibility of the scholars to preserve the knowledge left by others and also to preserve the knowledge which they themselves possess. Publication or reproduction in a form that will be available to others in the future is the foremost responsibility of the scholar. His enthusiasm for preservation of knowledge must be tempered with reason and judgment. Libraries and museums are, indeed, cluttered with much that is properly described as trash, or at least trivial. Age and uniqueness greatly change the value of simple objects. A kitchen knife of half a century ago is worthless, while an artifact of 25 centuries ago is a prized museum item. A phonograph record of Indian tales and songs by the last survivor of a now extinct tribe is carefully to be preserved. Although a few of our current phonograph records should be preserved, many of them are very doubtful items for preservation. Unless we can rapidly develop effective means for the miniaturizing of much of our published materials, we shall indeed have great difficulty in finding adequate storage space.

It is most important for the scholar to resist external forces that seek to select the nature of materials that should be preserved and the nature of materials that should be destroyed. Book burners and reformers have destroyed all copies of some documents, but many more times the courage of some scholar has preserved for civilization that which was the object of the purge.

The creation of new knowledge is the means by which the civilization of mankind progresses. The responsibility for the continual expansion of our knowledge is assumed by our scholars. With concentrated study of a particular field, one is led by curiosity and reflection to probe and explore beyond the work of others. Minor contributions and great discoveries are nearly always natural extensions of a systematically developing field of knowledge. It naturally follows that many discoveries are made simultaneously and independently in different parts of the world. No areas are closed to contemplation and exploration by the scholar, but there may be some restrictions on the release and publication of the results of his creative activity. In a very few fields, in the interests of public welfare, the degree to which the results of new discoveries can be published are limited by law. These limitations may affect such subjects, for example, as military security or nuclear energy. Fortunately these areas are steadily being reduced by declassification procedures. Quite irrespective of the legal restrictions that may exist, however, the scholar may be faced with serious questions of the moral responsibility for the unrestricted release of discoveries that may readily be put to undesirable or evil uses. Concealing this knowledge will not prevent its discovery by others in the course of time. In any case, the scholar should record fully his discoveries and take counsel with other scholars as to the restrictions that might appropriately be imposed by legal authorities.

There is a substantial difference between the initial conception of an idea and the proof of the idea or its development in physical form. Early Greek philosophers talked about atoms as units of matter, but this was a conjecture made without any evidence for its support. Jules Verne and other authors of science fiction have indeed described many devices and discoveries that now exist, but these authors cannot properly be said to be the inventors or discoverers of these devices. There are only a few cases in which an untrained mind has conceived a great idea or recognized an accidental discovery. The scholar is frequently annoyed by the discoverers of "unknown" and "undetectable" radiations or phenomena produced by "undetectable concentrations" of "critical elements" or by the discoverer of "new laws" and principles that claim to destroy the validity of most of modern science. Some scholars collect these items out of curiosity, while others destroy the material as worthless. Care must be exercised in this matter, since history records some cases where creative discoveries by amateurs have been initially rejected by the professionals.

The publication of unscholarly work and unjustified claims of priority of discovery are not confined to the untrained amateur but sometimes appear as contributions of scholars with established reputations. Scholars are indeed human and subject to the same failures of mental capacities as occasionally befall the average man. Such occasions are regrettable, but there is, however, a rather narrow line between brilliant and clear presentation and the illogical proposals and claims of a sick mind. It is the scholar's responsibility to study and analyze the work of others and where possible to verify the claims and observations reported. In this way we can best be assured of the truth and accuracy of the creative work of others.

The scholar shares with others a responsibility for the use of our accumulated knowledge and of the new discoveries and ideas that continually increase this store of knowledge. The preservation of knowledge and the creation of knowledge through research and discovery are activities that may have little direct relation to the society in which we live. Knowledge and discovery may indeed be pursued for their own sake, but there is an important responsibility for the scholar to use his knowledge and skills for the benefit of the society of which he is a part.

An intelligent society can be created only if the scholars will communicate the essential parts of their specialized knowledge to the general public, so that there can be general comprehension and appreciation of our intellectual progress. This is not a simple task, since many scholars are unable to express their ideas in language that can be understood by the interested lay citizen. In such cases we must encourage other scholars to serve as interpreters in translating the ideas and concepts from the technical and specialized forms used by the scholar into a simpler language that, although incomplete, will still develop some appreciation and respect in the public mind. It will be necessary to guide this activity so as to insure that the popular lecturer is himself a scholar and not an actor with a script.

The amount of support given to educational institutions by society through public tax support, tax exemptions, and private gifts will be proportional to the degree to which society appreciates the scholar's contributions to the general welfare. Active cooperation with those who seek to maintain the flow of scholarly knowledge to the general public is a double responsibility of the scholar. It is essential for the growth and development of the general society, and it is also essential as the means of encouraging public support of the facilities and subsistence required by the scholars. The possibility for scholarly work in many areas is wholly dependent on financial support from an enlightened society.

Although the scholar is not the guardian of society, nor is he directly answerable for the way in which his ideas or discoveries are used, he must, nevertheless, assume some responsibility.

When the scholar's greater knowledge and longer reflection about the consequences of the use of new information lead him to the conclusion that undesirable and injurious effects may result, it is, indeed, his responsibility to make this known to the public or to the appropriate officers of society. The discoverer of X rays was unaware of their harmful effects, but geneticists are now fully aware of the damage that can be done, and many scholars have recognized their responsible role to inform the public of these hazards. In the role of adviser and informer to the public, the scholar is often removed from the satisfying life of research and exploration and subjected to the less pleasant atmosphere of commercial and political discord.

The scholar welcomes discussion and debate with other scholars who are informed and competent in the matters under discussion. Although these specialists start with a substantial basis of accepted and established knowledge, they still may differ on the interpretation of new discoveries. Logic, reason, or experiment will usually settle the debate. Apparently scholarly pronouncements from outside the community of scholars, however, are often presented to the public and the press. There are, to be sure, some serious amateur scholars who are not wholly accepted by their professional colleagues; but these amateurs seldom seek the public press as the forum in which to present their discoveries or ideas. The more critical problems are presented by the fakers and charlatans and to a lesser degree the mentally unbalanced. These pretenders to knowledge may be more convincing and suave than the scholar. These pseudo-scholars are usually ignored by the true scholar, but this is unfortunately of small assistance to the public. Fraud or madness can often be confused with scholarship. The public-spirited scholar who diverts his efforts to the exposure of fraud is usually subjected to violent attack and occasional lawsuits if the enterprise he attacks has been a financially successful one. Some contend that the scholar is not the public guardian and urge a policy of *caveat emptor* for ideas as well as goods, but there is a much more convincing case to be made for the scholar's responsibility to protect society from dishonesty.

The man of learning is a skeptic in that he seeks to satisfy himself without the necessity for reliance on authoritarian pronouncements. The extent and complexity of our total knowledge is so great that the specialist in one area is usually not capable of checking or establishing the validity of pronouncements outside his own area of special competence. Because of this he must rely on his colleagues who have the ability to check such discoveries or statements. Superficially, this may seem to be a form of authoritarianism in which the authority of the group is accepted. But it is not a blind or unquestioned authority that is invoked, but rather one in which the arguments and evidence must be available for study and refutation. In the scholarly fields of experimental science authority must be based on competent observations. Mistakes or discoveries are identified with little difficulty. In the fields of sociology, economics, and political theory, it is far more difficult to establish the facts; and it is in this area that authoritarian doctrines are more likely to be used as the foundation for systems of social and political economy. With careful study, however, the faults and values of these authoritarian systems and doctrines can also be determined. Especially in matters of this nature the scholar has a responsibility to make his observations available to the public. The scholars who live in isolation from society have ceased to be a part of society.

The scholar's statements may be the object of analysis and study by his colleagues, but he is often quoted by the public and the press with respect for his authority. For this reason his quotable statements and interviews should be prepared with care. Facts established by observation should be differentiated from fancy and hypothesis. The battle with the press over out-of-context quotations selected to startle is one that the scholar cannot wage successfully against a sensationally oriented press. Where, however, the scholar's observations are quoted incorrectly or out of context to support a fraud or deception, it is clearly the scholar's responsibility to call attention to this error and to disclaim support of the enterprise.

In making available to society the benefits of increased knowledge, more is required than the publication of discoveries or ideas in scholarly proceedings. The translating of these publications into concepts that are understood by the public is essential. Also, in many technical areas there is an appreciable problem of development between the concept of an idea and the availability of articles of commerce. There continues to be a need for guidance from the scholar throughout this period of development, so that the full and effective benefits of the initial ideas are not lost or minimized in this transition.

The benefactions of others and the efforts of many help to provide and maintain the facilities that make possible the scholar's life in a productive atmosphere. Some of the responsibility for maintaining these institutions in a manner that is most agreeable for scholarly enterprise falls on the scholar himself. He must cooperate with the planners of our university communities in creating new facilities and in operating them with such controls as will be most effective in preserving them. This implies that some of the time and effort of the scholar will be spent in committee activities, and that administrative duties will be shared in turn. The advice and point of view of the scholar is required not only in the administration of our universities; they are also essential in the operation of our public and private foundations and agencies that support scholarly programs.

Active participation in politics is exceptional among our nation's scholars. Some presidents have sought the advice of college professors and many scholars have accepted temporary assignments to positions where their special knowledge was of unusual value to the country. Very few senators and representatives, however, have stepped from the professor's platform to the Capitol. And the numbers who do assist the government, through direct political or indirect bureau or department activity, do not represent an adequate participation of our best scholarship in the operation of our government, and through it our society. There is here also a real responsibility that should be met by the scholars of today.

The continuity of supply of scholars who will preserve, create, and use our knowledge is a responsibility of the scholars themselves. The selection of the apprentices for this profession must be wisely done so that the bright sparks of genius are given every encouragement. Strangely enough, our educational system tends to hold all students to a common and somewhat mediocre level of intellectual achievement in our secondary schools. The authoritarian society with which we are competitive today separates the potential scholars into different classes from the technicians and the workers. In their class society, the scholars are given assignments and opportunities that match their capacities and are in this way prepared for specialization when they enter their universities. In our universities the majority of the students devote an appreciable part of their time to the study of secondary-school subjects that were omitted from their preparatory program or were so badly taught that they must be repeated again. In addition to this they are usually required to take a broad program of arts, literature, philosophy, languages, history, social sciences, mathematics, and physical and life sciences with such a spread and dilution that they are poorly prepared for scholarly work in any specialized field. It is difficult to make a research scholar out of a French language major who knows no other language, or out of a physics major who knows no differential equations, or a political science major who knows no history. The scholar must play an active role not only in the selection of the apprentice scholar, but he must also see that the students' time devoted to studies is well spent. We shall not succeed in preparing the next generation of scholars if we continue a program of uniform education up to the time of college graduation. To say that specialization begins in the postgraduate period is equivalent to delaying the entrance of our students into scholarly research by at least two years. With limited facilities for the training of graduate students, it is most important that the procedures for the selection of these students be fair and effective. The failure to utilize unusual ability is probably more serious than the cost of effort spent on an inferior student. It would seem to be better policy to provide the facilities for enough graduate students so that in the end we have provided facilities that were used by a few students that failed to meet our standards of performance. Through supervision of a program of selection and training, the scholars can fulfill their responsibility for the provision of continuing generations of scholars.

FREEDOMS

A democratic society recognizes that each member has certain "natural" or, at any rate, "constitutional," rights that will be restricted only when he violates the rights of others. These rights are often defined as his *freedoms* and exist only when they may be exercised without fear of subsequent penalties. When arbitrary action deprives an individual of one of his freedoms, the group may fight for the restoration of freedom for all. Freedom designates the protected rights of an individual and cannot be said to exist when only those enjoy such rights as happen to be the defenders of dominant views. Responsibilities, however, are frequently a group obligation in which each member contributes his share of the total effort, with the integrated effort of all planned to meet the total responsibility. The fact that individuals do not contribute to each phase of the activity is not considered as an essential failure of the individual to meet his responsibilities.

It is probably the direct impact of restriction of freedoms on an individual that has made the rallying call for most of this nation's wars: "the fight for freedom"—"Life, Liberty, and the Pursuit of Happiness"—"Emancipation"—"Freedom of thought, freedom of worship, freedom from want, and freedom from fear." The call to battle in conflicts between scholars and administrators is in the defense of *academic freedom*. This is the assertion that the scholar, teacher and student both, shall have the freedom to study, teach, publish, and discuss that which they themselves consider to be appropriate to the field of their competence or study. Academic freedom exists only if these rights can be exercised without fear of punitive actions that will affect the present or future welfare of the scholar. It is sometimes stated that the freedoms for the scholar are simply the freedoms of thought and speech which all individuals claim, and that the scholar has no special rights that are not given to other citizens. The scholar has, in fact, no rights or immunities that other citizens do not possess, but he does have a substantially greater responsibility for the full exercise of these rights. It will be possible to develop an intelligent and creative society only if the scholars in our educational system plant and keep alive the freedoms of thought and speech. The freedoms of the scholar and those of the citizen are the same, but the importance and necessity for the forthright assertion of some of these rights may be more essential for the scholar. The general freedoms required for all members by our society may be expressed as *freedom to think, freedom to work, and freedom to live.*

Our democratic society has through the enactment of laws and through the force of generally accepted moral codes imposed restraints on its members. These limitations, however, do not limit the thoughts and beliefs of the individual. The right to think and believe must include not only the unexpressed inner contemplations of the individual but also the right to communicate to others these thoughts and beliefs. A teacher cannot properly present his subject if he is restrained in the expression of his own thoughts and beliefs. A student also must be free to express his opinions and beliefs. The faculty of one of the nation's larger universities recently passed a resolution advising its members that, unless required by law or the courts, the teacher should not answer the questions of government security investigators that ask the faculty for statements regarding a student's beliefs as revealed by classroom discussions or in conference with his teacher. The freedom to think includes not only the right of the individual to think and to believe; it also includes his freedom to communicate these thoughts to others.

In the scholar's pursuit of knowledge he must attack those artificial barriers that limit his freedom to work. Libraries, laboratories, and the materials with which he works must be freely at his disposal. He must be free to study, to teach, and to communicate with his colleagues by discussion and publication the results of his research and contemplations. Here also any restraints on the scholar are usually described as limitations of academic freedom.

Pursuit of knowledge in a democratic society must not be carried on solely by master-minded and centrally programed schedules. The privilege to work in a field may sometimes be regulated by society through a system of licenses, but the controlling agencies or societies must themselves be subject to controls that will prevent the power to license from becoming a force that stifles new ideas and creative work by the scholars in adjacent fields. Only through a free choice of pursuit for the scholar's activity can we obtain an unbiased or unregimented society itself. The quality of the scholar's contribution to the development of knowledge and his ability to develop new scholars will be primarily influenced by his freedom to perform his tasks.

The scholar with a creative mind requires the freedom to live his life in an environment and atmosphere that stimulate the development of creative ideas. The distractions arising from poverty and hardship and the strain of insecurity and fear are unsuitable for the scholar who seeks reflection and contemplation for the solution of difficult intellectual problems. While some may advocate a simple and austere life as best for the scholar, there should be no impediment to his seeking and enjoying an atmosphere of inconspicuous luxury if this stimulates his scholarly productivity.

TASKS AND OPPORTUNITIES

The responsibilities and freedoms of the scholar are ethical guides to his conduct and aspirations. His actual physical existence is, however, much more definitely determined by the tasks that are assigned him and by the opportunities that are available to him.

In our society a scholar is, with rare exception, dependent on employment in a university for his living. University officials assign to the scholar tasks which he is expected to perform in return for the payment of a regular salary. Although some of these assigned tasks become in time drudgery, the scholar accepts his chores because many of his assignments are compatible with his concept of his responsibilities. Teaching is the scholar's direct performance of his responsibility for the building up of a new generation of scholars. There is perhaps little intrinsic reward in this where time is spent with poorly prepared students who, though enrolled in the university, have no interest in scholarship. Serious students with ability and enthusiasm, however, can make the assigned task of classroom teaching a real pleasure. With our increasing demands for the education of a growing student population, it is becoming necessary to select more carefully the students who qualify for inclusion in the limited number that can be given a specialized education. This is especially true for schools or departments where endowments, faculty, or laboratories strictly limit educational capacity. Boards of admission, selection committees, and interviewing officers are primarily staffed by scholars from the university faculty. The selection and guidance of students are essential parts of the university program.

To preserve our knowledge it is necessary to have museums and libraries, and these institutions can be properly guided only by the scholars themselves. In the planning of campuses, construction of buildings, purchasing of equipment, books, and art objects, the scholar must contribute his proper share of time and effort to committee activities. Although the faculty complain of the loss of time involved in committee service, it would be an undesirable situation if the selection of books and equipment and the planning of laboratories and classrooms were left to nonacademic professional planners. This authoritarian operation of schools is not uncommon in our elementary and secondary schools, but it is seldom found in our universities. The inefficiency and occasional mistakes of faculty planning are more than compensated for by the contributions that the working scholars can make through their superior knowledge of the academic community.

Occasionally scholars are authorized by the university administration to serve on commissions or as consultants to federal or state agencies as a part of their academic assignments. In other cases they may be given permission to seek additional compensation for their services with public agencies or private industry. Through service as a consultant or adviser, the scholar is effectively making his specialized knowledge available to society. The contacts developed in this way often provide the professor with the understanding of current problems and discoveries that are developing in areas outside the university. Because of the substantial fees that are often paid for consulting services, problems sometimes arise when the university office is used as the headquarters for a consulting business.

The creation of knowledge through research should be a portion of the task assigned to all scholars by the university authorities. An institution that does not expect its staff to engage in research and does not provide the necessary time and facilities fails to qualify as a university. The provision of time for research should certainly not be limited to those faculty members who have secured government or private foundation grants and are able to purchase from the institution the release from other assignments. To undertake creative work, investigation, and exploration is seldom regarded by a scholar as a chore or task. For most scholars only time and other chores limit the effort that they devote to this activity.

The faithful completion of the tasks assigned by the scholar's "employer" represents the fulfillment of assigned obligations, but these do not measure or determine the scholar's responsibilities. The responsibilities we have described are not the invention of the administrative officers of the university. The realization by these officers of the general responsibilities of scholars will have a strong influence on the tasks that are assigned. Devotion to these responsibilities is an effective force in persuading the scholar to accept the tasks assigned, since he realizes that, in part through the tasks themselves and in part through his own efforts, he can make a substantial contribution to society's needs.

An ideal situation for the scholar will not be achieved, even in a society that fully recognizes the responsibilities and freedoms that are essential, unless he has the opportunity to pursue his intended program. Without time, facilities, and money at his disposal, the scholar will be nearly useless to society. Although he may live in an abstract world of thought, money is indeed the most necessary item for his academic as well as his physical existence. He may be free to pursue his research and investigations; but if the institution which provides him with a salary requires a heavy schedule of teaching and other duties, there may be little or no time left in which to exercise his freedom. If either the institution or the scholar were more adequately provided with money, the time for free pursuit of knowledge might become available.

Time and freedom are not the scholar's only requirements. Money is needed in increasing amounts to provide the facilities for his activities. An institution which provides its scholars with ample time for their activities can still fail through lack of money to provide adequate libraries, laboratories, and other facilities for research and teaching. Scholarly opportunities may, indeed, be limited even where the scholars are free to spend as they wish the library's meager funds. In the spiral of rising living standards and decreasing dollar values, it is not easy to determine the direction of our general support of facilities for the scholar's use. We appear to be spending large sums for the support of basic research in science. A bold scholar will now approach the federal government with a request for over 100 million dollars for his experiment, and he may quite possibly be granted a budget of 20 million a year for five years, with prospects of continued support at the same rate for an indefinite period. In spite of substantial support of this nature, we appear as a nation to be spending less per scholar in the measure of a commodity index based on the essentials required by the scholar. Although library book budgets increase, so have also the number of users and the costs of publication.

The life of a scholar should be pleasant. The satisfaction which he can experience from his work must not be lost through distractions and hardships. Here again adequate financial support can be very effective in providing the atmosphere of security and sufficiency. This freedom of life for the scholar does not imply a life of luxury, but rather a support that is adequate for his needs. Certainly a productive scholar should not have to seek nonscholarly employment in order to meet the day-to-day needs of his family. New ideas and concepts often come from periods of relaxed reflection and contemplation. The scholar's special needs frequently require that he work with books of his own, with collections of specimens, or objects of art. The creation of these surroundings requires not only an intelligent selection on the part of the scholar, but often the opportunity to travel in search of the items for his collection. In the same way in which a student finds that the personal inspiration of a good teacher cannot be replaced by books, the scholar finds that the personal exchange of ideas through conferences and visits adds much to the development of ideas that cannot be obtained from journals and correspondence. Here again the freedom to travel, to discuss, to collect, and to study may not be specifically restricted, but the practical use of these freedoms depends on the financial position of the scholar. Whenever the opportunity does not exist to utilize a freedom, that freedom itself is an illusion.

Time and discovery have not made appreciable changes in the responsibilities of the scholar nor in his necessary freedoms. The preservation, creation, and use of knowledge are nearly axiomatic for the scholar. The training of successive generations of scholars is a necessary corollary without which the continuation of scholars' responsibilities will not be possible. Substantial changes will continue in the development of the program of higher education which will change the methods of instruction and with this the tasks assigned to the scholar. The recent substantial progress achieved in scientific research has led to an appreciable increase in the funds provided for the support of further research. More important than this support has been an awakening of interest and appreciation of scholarship and the recognition that hard work and less play will be necessary if our students are to meet tomorrow's competition. We must determine at once if our low-priced, mass-production educational system is producing a new model with increased performance and endurance or just superfluous fins for a low-grade machine.

In the contest for funds from the public treasury and from private donors, it will be difficult to secure the financial support required to meet the scholar's responsibilities and to provide him with an adequate salary. In this century there has been a decreasing support per student in higher education when measured against our gross national product. The financial status of the professor relative to most other members of the community has at the same time become appreciably worse. The task ahead for the scholar is one of educating society so that there is genuine respect for scholarship.

6.

The University
and the Community

IRWIN T. SANDERS
Lecturer in Sociology
Harvard University

The American university often bewilders the visitor from abroad by its wide assortment of service bureaus, extension activities, and other seemingly nonacademic functions. To the uninitiated it may look suspiciously like the American drugstore, where products ranging from loaves of bread to dog leashes overshadow the pharmaceutical supplies which are supposedly the store's main reason for existence. But the extended activities of the American university have arisen in a definite social context, and they can only be understood and relevantly criticized if this larger social picture is borne in mind.

I

Every society has its central cultural themes, its accents or emphases in terms of which the lives of its members take on a common meaning. Some of these are contradictory at times; some are on the rise and others on the wane; but they all influence education in varying degrees. In the United States, the emphasis upon *bettering oneself* leads to social mobility by way of the educational ladder; the emphasis upon efficiency and success leads to many how-to-do-it courses; the accent upon egalitarianism means that courses are often paced at the speed of the mediocre instead of the unusually gifted student; the stress upon the pragmatic leads to concern for immediate problem solving rather than the accumulation of facts to be used "on a rainy day" when some need for them might exist.

One of these cultural themes which best explains the relationship between the university and its community is *the promotion of human welfare,* a theme that has been dominant since the early days of American history. The theme has taken different forms in different periods; in our own day it appears as the *service motif.* Any institution that wants to receive the continued support of the American people is likely to try to justify such support in terms of the service that it renders. It must do more than simply meet its obligation in a democratic society to be accountable to "the people." It must be accountable in a particular way: it must satisfy the people that it is making an active effort to extend and expand their welfare.

To see that the university is no exception, one must note how far-reaching and deep-rooted this service motif actually is. In the United States, as in many other countries, those in public office speak of themselves as *public servants.* They and their parties, when running for office, do not normally stress abstract ideals as much as they stress the actual benefits they have brought or intend to bring to their constituents. An important yardstick used by legislatures in determining the appropriations of money that go to public services is the amount of service rendered by an agency seeking funds. Such an emphasis, of course, is to be expected in a democracy; but its strength in the United States is sometimes quite surprising to those who tend to think of a governmental bureaucracy as relatively self-sufficient and self-perpetuating.

Americans, in short, live in a *welfare society* even though many of them resist the concept of a *welfare state.* Although the government is supposed to promote human welfare and to render many basic services, public opinion tends to support the continued existence of a strong sector of private, nongovernmental activity within which individual citizens and the groups of which they are a part also try to further human progress. Many projects—for example, the provision of public swimming pools and athletic fields, the care of crippled children, the maintenance of services for the aged or indigent—which in many other countries would be entirely left to local government, are sponsored by voluntary private citizens' groups. This may happen when the local government is not interested in such projects or is financially unable to handle them. But it may also happen out of the belief that private voluntary effort in such welfare areas is preferable to government activity.

The organized religious bodies similarly pay much attention to programs which minister to the needs not only of their own members but to those of the community as well. In the social medley that is America this *service* message is sometimes drowned out in the general clamor; but it can never be forgotten for long, for the minister, priest, and rabbi drive it home in their weekly homilies. Only rarely is religious teaching in the United States a teaching of meek acceptance; more often it urges positive action in a society where those who do not adhere to a specific religion will judge it by what it does rather than by what it says.

The American businessman, in his turn, is also likely to feel today, and usually quite sincerely, that his self-interest is best served if he actively subscribes to the ideal of promoting human welfare. Before the turn of the century a prominent industrialist could say with relative impunity, "The public be damned"; but today any such comment will almost certainly bring forth a hurricane of protest. The customer is the king and he demands service. A department store manager may accept with equanimity the charge that his prices are too high or that some of his products are not all that they should be; but he cringes when he is told that the service in his store is discourteous or bad. Automobile filling stations are known as *service stations;* utility repairmen who come to the house are known as *servicemen;* extra charges on one's bills are euphemistically called *service charges.* Even industrial concerns which may not deal directly with the public still pay lavishly to ensure that the public thinks of their enterprises as service-oriented.

Further evidence of the service motif is the existence throughout America of the so-called *service club.* This is likely to be a luncheon club which provides its members with an opportunity to enjoy congenial associations; but it will disguise this perfectly acceptable purpose under the label of *service,* and it is likely to do so whether its contributions to the community are large or small. And within most of these clubs there are individuals who devote an unbelievably large amount of their time to the service activities sponsored by these clubs. The fact that such activities may be paid for by the businesses with which these individuals are associated does not change, but reinforces, the conclusion that service is a dominant theme of American society.

The desire to render service, furthermore, prompts many Americans to think that promoting human welfare is a reward in itself and to choose occupations where economic rewards are low but these less tangible rewards high. The unprecedented development of philanthropic foundations in the United States is revealing testimony to this cultural theme. And it is only a step from this domestic surge of philanthropy to the sometimes willing, sometimes grudging support by tax-conscious Americans of foreign-aid programs. This also explains their shock, naïve at times, when they learn that there are those in foreign lands who do not view such programs as an expression of service, a desire to promote human welfare, but as an arm of American foreign policy that is quite devoid of any humanitarian overtones.

Higher education is part of this American scene in which the emphasis on service and progress is vocal, highly developed, and present throughout the nonpolitical aspects of life. An American university cannot wall itself off from the society which supports it, it must render service to that society or be considered alien and unworthy of the trust placed in it. Different universities differ in their interpretation of what service they should render, and various segments of the American public have varied expectations in this regard. But few of the commencement exercises which end the academic year ever conclude without a forthright statement from some responsible university spokesman about the great contribution his university is making to the welfare of the state or nation from which it draws its student body and its financial support.

II

An important embodiment of the service motif in higher education in the United States is found in the land-grant college. This is a uniquely American institution, but some of its features may have significance for other countries facing expanding technological, economic, and social frontiers. The land-grant college takes its name from the provision of the Morrill Act, passed in 1862 by the Congress of the United States, which set aside public land in each state, at the rate of 30,000 acres for each of its congressional representatives, for "the endowment, support, and maintenance of, at least, one college, where the leading object shall be, without excluding other scientific and classical studies, and including military tactics, to teach agriculture and mechanic arts . . . in order to promote the liberal and practical education of the industrial classes in the pursuits and professions in life." This grant of land was used to produce income to support the new colleges.

By 1879, forty-one institutions had benefited from these land grants. Six were private colleges: Rutgers, Vermont, Sheffield at Yale (to 1895), Brown (to 1892), Massachusetts Institute of Technology (mechanical arts), and Cornell; nineteen were state colleges or universities; ten were separate colleges for Negroes. By 1900, twenty-four colleges were added to the list of those benefiting from the land grants: five state universities, eight additional separate agricultural and mechanical colleges, and eleven more Negro colleges. Today there are seventy-two member institutions in the association of land-grant colleges and state universities.

The inspiration for the Morrill Act was the egalitarian philosophy advocated by Andrew Jackson which, in a sense, was a reaction against the aristocratic orientation of the higher educational institutions of the original thirteen colonies. Thomas Jefferson and others had considered such educational institutions to be selective agencies of society. A plan published in 1853 had a profound influence upon those who initiated and pushed through the Morrill Act. It was entitled *Industrial Universities for the People*, written by Jonathan Baldwin Turner, in which Turner maintained that the industrial classes ought to have the same facilities for understanding their pursuits as those enjoyed by the professional classes. In short, he argued for a people's university. And that is what the land-grant college started out to be and has to a considerable extent remained.

The early days following the American Civil War were difficult for these colleges, for comparatively few students were attracted to the new curricula and most of those who did attend were not adequately prepared for college-level work and had to be given some secondary schooling. Further difficulties were the lack of scientific knowledge relative to agriculture and some of the mechanical arts and the dearth of satisfactory books and teaching materials. This led to the development of the so-called "demonstration method," in which the instructor, by force of necessity, took students out into experimental garden plots or into machine shops to show them concretely what he had been lecturing about. Greater use of the laboratory was also a result.

The criteria for adding new subjects in land-grant colleges was not mainly derived from the traditions set by the medieval universities and kept alive in the older institutions in the Eastern states. Instead, the criteria was public demand or public utility. Isaac Roberts, a pioneer in the land-grant movement, teaching in the agricultural college at Cornell, recounts the following experience:

About 1888 a smiling young student approached me and asked me why we didn't have a poultry department. I replied rather sharply that I knew nothing about the chicken business; had no means to employ a man who did, if there was such a man; and that I had seen so many persons go through the chicken fever and come out looking like a moulting hen sitting on one egg, that I was in a critical frame of mind. Without being daunted in the least, he said that he knew something about the chicken business and would like to try his hand at it. He thought poultry culture ought to be taught at the college. He finally got me interested and I told him to draw up plans for a poultry plant. I proposed with our own hands we should build the first chicken house out of a great pile of refuse lumber left from an old barn.

Out of such incidents were the land-grant institutions fashioned. As time passed these institutions gained wide acceptance. They made demonstrable contributions to agricultural productivity and engineering skills; moreover, as the secondary schools spread from the cities to the rural counties, more young people, both boys and girls, became intellectually equipped for academic life; and more and more the curricula in the land-grant agricultural and mechanical colleges incorporated liberal-arts requirements. In many of these institutions strong English, history, and language departments developed alongside those in the biological and physical sciences and in engineering. Agricultural economics and rural sociology also received support. On the whole, and with exceptions at some points, the contemporary land-grant college provides those undergraduates who wish it as good a liberal arts education as many so-called liberal arts colleges. This is true whether the institution is a state university with an affiliated agricultural and engineering college supported by original land-grant funds or an entirely land-grant institution separated administratively and physically from the state university. In the land-grant institution, however, there is usually a strong tendency to take professional studies in the junior or senior year and to stress vocational subjects not ordinarily taught in most liberal arts colleges which follow the older traditions.

III

The primary function of the land-grant institutions, most of which have now assumed the title *university* instead of *college,* is to instruct the young people who work in residence for some academic degree. But there are other functions as well.

The University of Nebraska, for example, says that the entire state of Nebraska is the campus of the university. It is geared to serve not just the resident students but all of Nebraska, which is its community. In this view of its functions it is fairly typical of other land-grant universities. To carry out this purpose special administrative structures have been devised on a national scale. These give the land-grant institution a threefold emphasis as far as its agricultural college is concerned. In addition to the resident instruction already mentioned, there are at each such institution an agricultural experiment station and the headquarters for the state agricultural extension service.

The agricultural experiment stations were established under the provisions of the Hatch Act of 1887 and given additional support under the Adams Act of 1906 and the Purnell Act of 1925. These acts make possible the contribution of federal funds to be used along with state funds to support the study of problems affecting farming and farm people. One explanation for the phenomenal increased productivity of American agriculture has been the existence in each state of a research facility which has investigated the problems of immediate concern to the farmers of that state and, at the same time, has carried on types of basic research that had application elsewhere. The staff members of these agricultural experiment stations originate research projects; these are reviewed locally and are then reviewed in Washington to qualify them to receive federal funds. Once the grant is made there is much local autonomy and no federal interference in the methods used or the types of findings to be publicized. To a surprising degree, the spirit of free inquiry prevails.

The third aim of the agricultural college is that of agricultural extension. This activity offers the services of a specially trained staff to take to farmers and housewives the results of the research carried on in the experiment stations and elsewhere so that these findings can be applied to the daily tasks of the farm and the household. To this end, most of the 3,050 counties in the United States have a county agent, who works with farmers, and a home-demonstration agent, who works with housewives, in what is essentially an educational program. Many counties, in addition, have an assistant county agent who works with rural youth. These agents are paid partly by federal funds, under the provisions of the Smith-Lever Act of 1914 and the Bankhead-Jones Act of 1936, partly by state funds, and partly by local county funds. Local officials are not forced to take any agents whom they do not want; but their nominees must be approved by the state director of extension at the land-grant college, who is in a position to evaluate their technical competence. The federal government, as its part in the Co-operative Extension Service, assists in the general training of these extension workers through conferences and the preparation of materials; essentially, however, they are under the supervision of the state staff. Also headquartered at the land-grant college are a number of subject-matter specialists in fields like poultry, horticulture, animal husbandry, agricultural economics, etc., whose chief task is to help the county and home demonstration agents in their specialties. In almost every county of each state, therefore, there are qualified workers who, though responsible to local officials, are also staff members of the land-grant college. In this sense the state really is the campus of the university.

But there are numerous other ways, in addition, in which the land-grant institution renders service. Annually it holds a Farm and Home Week on its campus to which hundreds and even thousands of rural people from all over the state come in order to hear lectures, see demonstrations, and otherwise learn not only more of the world around them but also about newer techniques to be used on the farm or in the kitchen. Each land-grant college also gives periodic short courses, varying from two to six weeks in length, which are attended by those who desire detailed information about some phase of farming. During the Farm and Home Week, and even in some of the short courses, many social as well as economic aspects of life are treated. For example, the rural church or rural cooperatives and other organizations often figure prominently in the programs presented; in addition, short courses have been offered to ministers of any faith or to organizational leaders who work with rural people and who want to know more about changes under way in rural life.

Just as the agricultural college has served rural people, so the mechanical (now engineering) colleges have served industry. Their most important contribution has been to train a large portion of the technical staff without which American industry could not have progressed as it has. Research projects in land-grant universities have investigated problems of mining, metallurgy, highway construction, machine design, and fuel efficiency which have been of immediate, practical interest to industrialists of the state concerned. While not supported nationally by any federal department as strong as the Department of Agriculture, these engineering colleges have, nevertheless, been able to get grants from a variety of sources to underwrite the research they have considered necessary. They have not had the occasion to set up an extension system comparable to that serving agriculture, but they have maintained close liaison with industry, since many professors move out of academic chairs to positions in industry and back again.

The land-grant institutions have increased in size and in financial resources chiefly because they have been ready to incorporate into their curricula bodies of knowledge which people have wanted taught. Now and then this has been carried to what many would think a ridiculous extreme; but it has been justified by the university authorities concerned on the basis of the service being rendered rather than on the basis of abstract canons of academic respectability. The undoubted extremes to which some institutions have gone should not blind one, however, to the solid core both of humanities and science to which most students are exposed in the land-grant institution. Whether this exposure takes the student out of a narrow vocational interest and makes him a better informed and all-around person will depend upon the quality of such studies as well as their duration. And around this point much debate about higher education in the United States rages today.

IV

Another form of publicly supported institution is the so-called state university. Although twenty state universities have no land-grant connection, they have, nevertheless, been strongly influenced by the land-grant philosophy. In these twenty states (for instance, Alabama, Kansas, Washington) the state legislature is faced with the task of appropriating public funds to provide for the maintenance of both the land-grant and the state university. As indicated earlier, the argument for support of the state university is based not mainly upon its resemblance to the old, private Ivy League colleges but upon the contribution it is making to the citizens of the state in which it exists. This has forced many state universities into a kind of competition with land-grant institutions which they might prefer to avoid; but it has also brought them into closer touch with the people of their states.

The devices for serving the people of the state are now found in all the state universities, whether land-grant or not, and, indeed, even in many private universities. These devices are of several types. One of the most prominent is the department of university extension, which is entirely separate from the "agricultural extension program" mentioned earlier. University extension is concerned with a wide array of activities which bring the university's resources into the life of the people. First, there are correspondence courses which have been prepared by the university staff, and which are given official university credit even though the student has not been in class attendance. Most universities limit the number of such courses which an individual may count toward a degree; a large number of people who may not be interested in a degree, however, can delve more deeply through such correspondence courses into some area of knowledge. The postman brings the university to the door. The same department of university extension may also maintain adult education centers in selected cities throughout the state, and offer courses taught personally by university staff members. These correspond in content to the same courses that are taught on the university campus, although the time and place of meeting may prevent the student from attaining an equal mastery of the materials. The department of university extension may also operate a speakers' bureau through which community groups can procure some university staff member as a speaker. Many of the more popular professors are written to directly by such groups; but those contacted through university extension also go only on their own terms. Needless to say, the university authorities think it good public relations as well as good educational practice to have their staff members appear throughout the state, for the university's interest in the larger community it serves can be made manifest in this fashion.

The department of university extension is apt to devote much of its energy, too, in working with the high school students of the state. It may provide debating materials and stage a state-wide debating contest on the university campus; or it may do the same for oratory, singers, bands, or single instrumentalists. It may even arrange for instruction in baton-twirling or cheer-leading at athletic events and assist the athletics department in bringing hundreds of youngsters to some heralded athletic event to perform during intermissions. Through such efforts the university hopes to interest the most promising young people in choosing it as their alma mater, and to convince the parents of these young people that the university has their interest at heart.

But this by no means exhausts all the responsibilities of the department of university extension. Many such departments have extensive film libraries. These films may be employed by the university's instructors for classroom use on the campus; but they are also shipped out by the scores each day to civic groups, high schools, and other interested parties at low rental fees. Quite a few such departments have specialists to help the officers of various organizations with their problems, as well as specialists in community organization who advise community leaders about ways in which to deal effectively with community problems of serious concern. The net result of all such endeavors is to apply the knowledge, supposedly reposing in the university, to the everyday situations which ordinary people face.

A second device which links the university with the community is the research and service bureau. Almost every college of the university is apt to maintain such an agency. The college of education may staff and run a bureau of school service which conducts educational surveys in the state and advises school board members and school administrators on a wide variety of technical problems. The college of commerce or business administration may have a bureau of business research which investigates theoretical and practical problems dealing with the economy of the state. A bureau of government research may render assistance to local governments needing fiscal or other advice, not in any effort to compete with or eliminate professional private consultants in this field, but simply to make the resources of the university more generally available to those who believe they can benefit from them. In many universities such bureaus exist in fields like social welfare, recreation, psychological testing, public health, applied arts, family counseling, journalism—to mention a few. The net effect of such services has been to habituate the citizenry in many states to turn to their state university, be it land-grant or not, when they have some problem they want answered. It has also kept the academician who is involved in these services more steadily aware of the level of knowledge and the developing interests of the people of his state.

There is another important way in which the university also renders service. It maintains laboratories or technical staffs which serve state agencies rather than individuals. The geological survey program in a given state may be housed at the state university and be affiliated with it; similarly, the laboratory which examines animal heads for rabies, the bureau which tests seeds and fertilizers, or highway-materials testing laboratory may all be a part of the total university enterprise which can be used as convincing talking points when the university's administrators seek additional funds from state legislatures. Latin and Greek, though a part of the educational scheme of things, do not have the practical appeal to legislators, it is plain, which other aspects of the university possess. Indeed, part of the job of a state university president today is to safeguard and even enhance the humanities and theoretical sciences while at the same time emphasizing the applied activities of his institution in seeking statewide support.

V

The private college and university, which is not supported by government funds, does not duplicate all the services of the public university. But it too fills an important niche in the pattern of community service. Its community is not defined by state boundaries, for it need not go to a state legislature for financial support. If it is church-supported, then its appeal is not only to those in its immediate local community but to a larger religious body. If it is an independent nonsectarian institution, attached neither to church or state, it must depend on tuition, endowment, alumni gifts, and foundation grants to maintain its standards of performance. From the standpoint of American society as a whole, private institutions, like the state universities, have the fundamental function of preparing well-qualified students for later positions of leadership and trust. Private institutions, to be sure, can no longer claim a monopoly or even unchallenged leadership, in training the professional man; but they do argue effectively when they speak of preserving the liberal arts ideal in an age when it is in danger of being overshadowed by other concerns. Their relative independence of public funds puts private institutions in a unique position to exert an influence out of proportion to the size of their student bodies. Dr. Nathan M. Pusey, President of Harvard University, in speaking at the inauguration of a state university president on September 26, 1958, urged that "we talk less about what the university can do for the state, and ask rather more frequently, seriously, and consistently, what can our states do to strengthen their universities for their essential tasks." The most important of these tasks is the promotion of scholarship. And although Dr. Pusey recognizes that a wide variety of institutes, clinics, and research activities of immediate practical significance may have a vital place within the university, he is concerned that the university's fundamental task—scholarship—not be sacrificed to the pressures of the immediate and the practical.

Even those institutions where the ideal of pure scholarship is most revered are not free, however, from the influence of the service motif epitomized by the land-grant college. Along with other institutions they cooperate with the International Co-operation Administration, for example, in sending qualified staff members to other countries; or a team of specialists may go overseas from such an institution to organize an institute of business administration, a social science research unit, a public health laboratory, or to train university librarians. In a sense, the world has become the university community with which the scholar shares his knowledge and skills.

The private university also illustrates along with the state university an additional characteristic of higher education in America. American business, industrial, political, and professional leaders tend to turn to the university when they have problems to solve; much of the research which such leaders require is done in university laboratories and research units, therefore, instead of in research institutes set up under other auspices. Such research is as much a job of any major American university as teaching, although the two complement and strengthen each other. Wherever one looks, in other words, one finds the American university of whatever type closely linked with the total society of which it is a part. Different demands are made upon different types of institutions, for they do not have the same resources or represent altogether the same intellectual interests. But this variety represents one of the strengths of higher education in America.

Some institutions are able to resist undesirable influences; others advance to new and useful forms of activity while their sister institutions are mistakenly trying to hold the line. One guarantee of continued vitality in American education, indeed, is the frequency with which qualified scholars move from one type of university to another, judging each institution on its own merits, and choosing their activities without reference to the type of financial support—i.e., public or private—which their university receives.

VI

This brings us to a fundamental issue. In the academic setting which exists in most American universities a professor plays different roles at different times. He is alternately a teacher, a researcher, an administrator, and an interpreter of knowledge. The importance which a professor attaches to each of these roles will be connected with the reference groups from which he seeks approval and in terms of which he judges what is appropriate and inappropriate professional conduct.

The professor who makes the student body his reference group often develops into a popular, provocative lecturer upon whom the undergraduate groups shower whatever honors they have at their disposal. Such a professor, with whom the teacher role is primary, focuses his interest on the classroom and derives most of his satisfactions from student response. The professor whose reference group is his professional colleagues, those working in his own or allied disciplines, may concentrate more upon the laboratory or library than upon the classroom. The slogan "publish or perish" may stand for nothing more than an economic or social imperative; but it may also express the scholar's commitment to a way of life on which his most fundamental personal values depend. In his choice of problems to be studied, such a scholar may or may not take into account those of immediate public concern or those for which foundation or other financial support is readily available. He may or may not agree to work as part of a research team. But he is more interested in advancing knowledge than in interpreting what others have found, whether in the classroom or elsewhere. Many of those professors who accept this as their paramount role may show little concern about the university and the community. They consider the world of scholarship as their community.

Since a modern university is so diverse in its interests and complex in its operations, some people, however, have to devote much of their time to the administrative machinery involved. Those professors who take the whole university community— and not their own subject-matter colleagues—as their reference group may begin to behave "politically" in the hope that those who have responsibilities to share will choose them for various tasks. This usually begins with strategic committee assignments and leads them through the hierarchy up to deanships, vice-presidencies, and the presidency of the university itself. Those who fall in this category are likely to spend long hours preparing reports instead of scholarly publications; they originate and direct the bureaus set up for many purposes; and they are sensitive to public relations problems between the university and its community, local, state, or national. At a certain level of administration, such men step out of the professor's role. They no longer have time to teach, though they may wistfully put themselves down for a seminar in the hope that they may be able to work it into their busy schedules. Yet there are many tasks dealing with university administration still left for those who are bona fide professors but who show an interest in keeping the social machinery of the university running in high gear.

The larger community outside the university itself often becomes the reference group of many professors who seek to play the interpreter role. They enjoy dealing with nonacademic men of affairs and welcome the opportunity to explain or speak about their academic specialty to various lay groups. In fact, they may attach more importance to testifying learnedly before a congressional committee than to reporting research to their national professional association. They become prominent in various national organizations which are frequently quite unrelated to their academic discipline; they write for the popular magazines but think of themselves as professors interpreting some fact of knowledge to those needing it. Numbered in this group are those who work in the applied fields of science or the humanities, particularly when they view the opportunity as one of interpreting in practical ways the value of the subjects which they teach and in which they do research.

Most university professors, of course, perform more than one of these roles. And the existence of these multiple roles attached to the status of university professor affects both the professor and the community. From the professor's standpoint he is constantly being confronted with difficult alternatives. In the days when teaching and research were all that mattered, life was cut in a much simpler mold; when the professor becomes involved in the operation of the complex university of today, or is expected to be an interpreter of knowledge for the general public, he finds insufficient hours in the day. The system of granting sabbatical leave helps him shift from the teaching to the research role, but there is no comparable arangement whereby he can control his administrative responsibilities. He either does them poorly and is not asked to do them again, with certain possible consequences in rank and salary, or he does them so well that his other roles are seriously restricted. And if he is forced into the interpreter role for too long a time, he may lose the sustaining power of serious scholarship and run dry.

Each professor, therefore, has to work out the combination of roles he finds most congenial and to sort out his relations with the various reference groups that play upon the academic life.

Certain tasks are bread-and-butter ones and must be performed to keep the courses and research projects moving along; others present dilemmas which have to be resolved by the individual himself. This variety of roles, distracting though it is, is by no means entirely negative in its influence. There can be a stimulating carry-over from the role of extramural interpreter to the role of teacher in the classroom; research ideas may develop from committee experience in which ideas have been exchanged with someone from a completely different college or discipline. To the extent that the individual can unify the experience gained in these various roles, to that extent he becomes a more effective professor in an American university.

The multiplicity of roles also has implications for the community at large. No longer is it possible to stereotype the professor as neatly as formerly. Professors are playing several roles; they move from the campus to the larger community; they mix the practical with the theoretical; they write learned treatises but they also write pocketbooks—and pocketbooks of quite respectable intellectual quality—that sell by the score at the corner drugstore. Some even run for office and get elected to Congress; others are asked to serve as directors of industrial concerns; still others take foreign assignments of various sorts for the United States government. Although students may see a well-known professor in a large lecture hall twice a week, they may also be aware of the many other things he is doing as a public service to his university or to the world of scholarship at large.

This is a desirable result in contemporary America where there is still a lingering suspicion of the intellectual. An increasing contact between the university and the community can bring about a better accommodation, if not a complete understanding, between intellectual groups and other groups. Nor do such activities mean that the rigorous pursuit of scholarship must be weakened or that the plaudits of the hustings and the market place must replace the firm standards of those who are com-

mitted to seek the truth honestly and to live with the difficulties
that are inherent in genuine intellectual inquiry.

VII

Are there lessons that emerge from this brief examination of
the university and the community in the United States today?
Whether one rejoices in the fact or not, American higher education has been a curious mixture of two quite different educational
philosophies and pedagogical procedures. One, represented in
the oldest private universities, has stressed the pursuit of scholarship as an end in itself and has sought to instill into each
successive college generation a *humane* approach to life as the
best possible preparation for adulthood. A second philosophy,
in contrast, has insisted that scholarship be placed directly at the
service of the people and that educational efforts be directed not
only at dignifying the lowly vocations but at dignifying the
individuals concerned. Not just the gentleman but the man who
grew the gentleman's food must share in the educational heritage
of his society. These two philosophies continue to clash and the
differences between them may never be fully resolved. But they
revitalize each other.

American democracy probably would not have developed as
we know it today if higher education had remained the exclusive
prerogative of the nobly born or of those able to pay high tuition
fees. The American economy would probably not have experienced as rapid industrialization, mechanization, and ration-
alization if land-grant colleges had not taught the necessary
skills and had not done so in such a way that those acquiring
these skills did not consider themselves to be second-rate citizens
being given a less desirable educational experience. The American class system, which is predominantly a middle-class system,
has come about, in part at least, because most American young
people could acquire a college degree if they wanted it badly

enough. This degree, which one symbolized upper-class status, is now the possession of ever larger numbers. Yet its wide distribution, because of the utilitarian strain in higher education and an economy to match, has not produced the problem of the unemployed intellectual which is found in many countries where a university degree divorces its holder from anything technical or nonprofessional.

There is no simple guide to understanding American higher education and no complete consistency of pattern or organization or outlook. The common theme of rendering service is a powerful binding force, but different institutions interpret differently what kind of service they should render. They also differ in their definitions of the community they serve; some stress the immediate locality, others the state, and others the community of scholarship. Finally, the professor finds himself confronted with an assortment of roles, all legitimate in the university setting, but some more congenial to his tastes than others. The net effect of the trends of the past decades, however, has been to make the university (and its professors) more aware of the existence of nonacademic publics which the university may and should serve; and these trends have also made these supporting publics more cognizant of, and more friendly to what the university has to offer. Thus far, to be sure, public expectations with regard to universities remain somewhat different from the academic standards which universities set for themselves. But those responsible for higher education in the United States hope that the gap can be closed by raising public expectations to the standards held by the professors themselves. For scholars, though they need not be afraid of the practical and applied, still realize that the rigorous search for truth has an urgency and an interest of its own and that it requires an arduous discipline which it is the primary function of a university in any society to exemplify, to defend, and to extend.

7.

In Loco Parentis: University

Services to Students

ROBERT M. STROZIER

President
The Florida State University

When I was Dean of Students at the University of Chicago, a Frenchwoman who taught at a lycée visited the campus. When I was presented to her, she asked, *"Mais qu'est-ce que c'est qu'un Dean of Students?"* I replied as fully as possible, explaining the concern of my office for the total life of the student. I explained our interest in seeing that the life outside the classroom be meaningful so that each student might fully realize his potentiality, both as a student and as a citizen. I attempted to show her that this interest did not bespeak paternalism or the desire to mold the young mind to a particular pattern of thought, but, on the contrary, was an attempt to free the mind for independent thinking. When I finished my explanation, she asked sweetly, *"Mais est-ce important?"*

I have often pondered that question.

Visitors from abroad who come to study in the United States are almost universally critical of the extent of the services, particularly the counseling services, available to American students. Those students from abroad who enroll in independent colleges are almost always irked and annoyed by the structural life of these institutions.

In one sense these visitors are correct in assuming that college life on the American campus breeds conformity instead of independence. They are also correct in the judgment they often express that intellectualism is not an American ideal, despite the great contributions of the American academic community to the realm of knowledge, particularly in the natural and the social sciences. The comic representation of the absent-minded professor, which flourishes in the United States, and the fact that "braintruster" and "egghead" are terms of opprobrium do not escape their notice.

Again, the campus of the American college[1] is unique. The classrooms in which the teaching is done form part of a larger community which includes libraries, an administration building, the chapel, a hospital, a football stadium, a student union building, dormitories, and rows of fraternity and sorority houses. Many campuses also include apartments or houses for married students.

To many, the existence of such things in an intellectual community seems strange and foreign. But these services, buildings, campuses, and administrative mechanisms have causes and functions, and one must understand what they represent before one can understand why they exist.

I

Prior to entering college, the average American student has spent eight years in an elementary school and four years in a high school. Although there are many private schools which replace the public high school, these are usually reserved for those who can afford them or for students who have some family or personal reason which makes it advisable for them not to live at

---

[1] The term *college* rather than *university* is used throughout this chapter because there are many four-year colleges which stand apart from universities, while all universities in the United States have at their base a college of arts and sciences. In the college, the student prepares for the bachelor's degree in arts, sciences, engineering, business, and a variety of other subjects. After receiving the bachelor's degree, the student may continue research for a master's or doctor's degree or enter a professional school, such as law, medicine, etc.

home and attend a public high school.

The modern American high school reflects, on a minor scale, many aspects of the college campus. There are usually athletic teams, theatrical groups, a newspaper, student government on a limited scale, a band, a glee club or choir, and there is counseling, guidance, and testing. During the third, or junior year of high school, students are given objective tests, such as those given nationally by the Educational Testing Service, to assess their latent academic talents. To these tests are often added others which enable a student to define more accurately his vocational interests. With the results of these tests in hand, a counselor discusses with the student the choice of a college as well as the choice of a career. Representatives of many colleges call at the high school and are available for personal conferences with interested students. The student makes a formal application to the college or colleges of his choice during the autumn of his senior year in high school.

The American college signifies its interest and concern for the individual student the moment he files a formal application for admission. Even before this, the prospective student has probably received printed material concerning the special characteristics of the institution, has perhaps been interviewed personally by a representative of the school, and has probably discussed with the counselor in his secondary school the advantages of a variety of schools. The formal application, indeed, may not even signify that the student has made his choice, for multiple applications to colleges have become common practice in the mid-twentieth century. As a typical result of this practice, one of the most respected colleges in the United States accepts 1,800 applicants each year in order to be assured of a freshman class of 1,200 students who will actually accept the offer of admission.

The completed application includes information concerning the student's academic performance in high school, his reputation as attested by his principal or adviser, his curricular and extra curricular interests and accomplishments, his marital status, his financial status, his physical attributes, and his vocational objective. Many schools also require a picture of the applicant as well as information concerning his religious preference; but such requirements are no longer part of the application forms employed by many schools, which attempt to avoid discrimination on the basis of race or religion. In accepting the student, the college, therefore, has already made several important decisions. It believes the applicant will fit into the particular climate of the institution, that he has a reasonable chance to succeed academically, and that he will be a good citizen of the academic community.

When he enters college the following autumn, the student enters a bright new world. His leaving for college, to begin with, usually means his first real break with his close family relationships. Upon being graduated from college, most students do not attempt to reenter the family scene on the intimate terms which had previously existed. The American college graduate, male or female, normally expects, on the contrary, to enter graduate or professional school or to begin work immediately after graduation. The spinster daughter who neither works nor makes any organized contribution to community life has almost passed from the American scene.

The new student, or freshman, spends his first week on the campus in what is commonly called *orientation*. During this period he meets his counselor for conferences about his academic program, is introduced to the many facets of extracurricular life, attends several social affairs, and starts making an adjustment to life in a new environment. The "main show," the classes, are, of course, under the central academic tent. But the side shows of whose existence the student learns are many and varied. In general, they are presided over by an official, known as the Dean of Students, the Dean of Men, or, in some cases, the Assistant Dean of the College.[2]

The University of Chicago, which first established an office of Dean of Students, defines the position in these terms:

In addition to the (academic) Deans . . . there shall be a Dean of Students of the University. . . . He coordinates the University's relations with students, including admissions, recording and reporting, health service, physical education and athletics, the educational and social supervision of residence halls and clubhouses, the direction of social affairs, the control of student organizations and publications, vocational guidance and placement, student aid, the administration of fellowships and scholarships, and of the service function of the Office of Examinations, and of student advisory service in the College, the Divisions, and the Schools. He is an ex officio member of all committees on the curriculum in the College, the Divisions, and the Schools.

Definition of the terms contained in this statement presents a reasonably accurate account of the services provided by American colleges to their students.

Admissions reflects the activities of the office of admissions. Representatives of this office have the first associations with prospective students when they visit high schools in order to explain the nature of their college and the particular characteristics of its academic program. The student who is accepted has received a formal certificate of admission from this office before he arrives to enter the college.

Recording and reporting indicates the registrar's office, where all official academic records are kept.

Health services include a complete physical examination, required of each new student during his first days on campus, hospital care for the student when he is ill, medical advice when

---

[2] The title, Dean of Students, first used about 1930, has become current in almost all areas of the United States with the exception of the Northeast.

he asks for it, and psychiatric consultation for students who are maladjusted or, perhaps, for those involved in disciplinary problems. Health services also have the responsibility to maintain a complete record of the student's health and physical condition.

Physical education and athletics involve a variety of activities which occasion a continuing, lively discussion inside and outside the United States. Most colleges require formal physical exercises and games during the first and second years. Further, only a few American colleges do not have athletic teams which represent them in intercollegiate competition. Football is king of these sports, probably as a result of a combination of factors. It presents an interesting spectacle during the most delightful season of the year—the autumn. Bands in colorful costumes, and cheerleaders who perform like acrobats add to the spectator's interest during the interval at the midpoint of the contest. The game itself is rapid and easily understood. Its place on the college scene generates complicated issues. The methods by which outstanding players on high school teams are recruited for the best college teams have been the subject of controversy and have led to the censuring of certain colleges; yet the system persists. And while there has been some waning of keen interest in football in the Northeastern colleges, this has in no way affected the Midwest, the West, and the South. Students may also participate in intercollegiate teams in basketball, baseball, tennis, golf, swimming, and other sports, and in intramural teams of many kinds.

The educational and social supervision of residence halls and clubhouses clearly indicates that the college assumes that the residence halls and clubhouses have educational goals. For this reason there are residence-hall counselors who live in the dormitories with the students, just as there are social and educational advisers in the student unions and clubhouses and in the fraternities and sororities.

The new student is assigned a room in a dormitory before he arrives at the college, and his residence-hall counselor is likely to be the first person to greet him when he arrives. Since the counselor lives in the dormitory, he is available for conferences or advice at almost all hours of the day or night. Freshmen are almost always required to live in the official residence halls maintained by the college. Afterward, however, the student normally has a choice. Some prefer to join fraternities during their freshmen year and after becoming members, to live in the fraternity house during their remaining years in college. However, the college also assumes responsibility for the general supervision of such groups.

The clubhouse or student union is the general center of student activities. Dances, teas, and parties are held in the union, and many clubs and activities have offices assigned to them there by the director of the union.

The direction of social affairs includes coordinating social affairs like dances, teas, or meetings with visiting dignitaries, assuring proper chaperonage for parties which include both sexes, and contriving group activities which will attract those who are timid and lonely. In some cases it also includes devising subtle means of improving the dress and manners of those who obviously need advice in these matters. In the larger colleges, and particularly those affiliated with universities, the direction of social affairs is mainly a matter, however, of supervising the scheduling of social events to avoid conflicts.

The control of student organizations and publications presents the Dean of Students with many problems. Glee clubs, debating societies, and interest clubs are somewhat peripheral to the central organization, the student government. Student government has grown in importance, particularly since World War II and the National Student Association, which coordinates the activities of the student governments of several hundred colleges has become an organization of importance. The degree of importance and independence accorded to the student government and the student newspaper reflects the degree to which a college's administration follows or does not follow a paternalistic policy.

Vocational guidance and placement are available to all students of the college. Advisers provide tests for students who wish advice on their career objectives, and the office of vocational guidance and placement assists the student in his last year to find a suitable position after graduation. This office also keeps credentials on file for those who request the service so that these credentials may later be referred to prospective employers.

Student aid has become increasingly important in the college scene. Harvard College, for example, has assumed a leading role in assisting the student and his family to assess his financial obligations for the four years of college. The plan of combining the resources available to the student from his family with some scholarship assistance from the college, or with part-time work on the campus or in the community, has come to be generally accepted by students and the public.

The administration of scholarships and fellowships is more important in the private than in the state colleges, but has importance in all colleges. Colleges supported by the states charge small fees, while the tuition in private colleges has steadily increased. In 1958 a charge of $1,000 a year for tuition in a good private college is not considered excessive, and several Eastern schools charge as much as $1,300. When one adds to this the cost of living, clothes, transportation, and books, and supplies, the price of attending many private colleges ranges from $2,500 to $3,000 a year. These rising costs have greatly increased the scholarship aid necessary to and available for many superior students. Private individuals and large corporations are increasingly awarding grants to colleges for their scholarship programs. In addition, the large foundations and such quasi-governmental agencies as the National Science Foundation provide fellowships at the graduate level.

Student advisory service is the most complex of all the services of the college. It includes academic counseling in choosing a course of study, assessing a student's progress from time to time, diagnosing the reasons for his failure or lack of progress, and guiding him in the ultimate choice of his major interest. It may also include personal counseling in the residence halls or by a psychologist or psychiatrist, by a college chaplain, or the workers of the religious faiths represented at the college, by a social counselor, or by a member of the faculty who is not officially a counselor.

As will be seen from this catalogue of special services which American colleges offer their students, there is an undeniably paternalistic atmosphere in the American collegiate scene. Indeed, it may seem incongruous that a nation that contains many citizens who express misgivings about the concept of the welfare state should accept and foster colleges which immerse the student-citizen in welfare services that affect almost every phase of his college life. But this paternalism has aspects and causes which must be understood even if we remain unconvinced, in the final analysis, that it is wholly defensible. In most American colleges, the students reside in the college community rather than at the residence of their parents. The typical American undergraduate severs the home tie at the age of eighteen, and his shift to a new intellectual climate is combined with a shift to a new climate of authority in which something must replace the home and the church. A Dean of Students who stands *in loco parentis* is a natural response to such a situation. Furthermore, it must be remembered that, as a general rule, the student's use of his college's service is a matter for his own discretion. No one forces him to seek advice, counsel, and services except in the case of serious emotional or physical illness. Though deans of students stand *in loco parentis*, they exist not to keep the student in a dependent attitude, but to aid in the process by which young people can move on to full status as active and understanding participants in democratic processes.

II

Foreign observers often wonder why the government of the United States does not pass laws which would make sensible the present, confused academic terminology; why it does not provide the funds for free higher education for all qualified students, why it does not close the doors of those colleges which lack the faculty, laboratories, and equipment to provide a good education to their students, why it does not provide a realistic public appraisal of colleges and universities and grade them just as it requires that food and clothing be marked honestly. And foreign observers often ask with a peculiar emphasis whether American colleges must inevitably continue to serve parental and familial functions as well as strictly intellectual ones.

Traditions are established unintentionally, but they have a force and function none the less—a setting, in Taine's words, designed by *la race, le moment, le milieu.* Centralized control of education is unthinkable in the United States. The diversity in size, quality, quantity, and type of financial support is the hall-mark of the American system of higher education and is firmly ingrained in the mores of our people. Millions of Americans pay taxes which support state universities and local junior colleges, while at the same time enrolling their children in private institutions where costs are relatively high. Their reasons for doing so are personal and are not subject to question without encroaching on the terrain of what they regard as personal liberty. Thus, higher education in the United States, in fact, is a responsibility that falls on various shoulders; the people, the states, or churches all have this responsibility. A religious sect may found a college and insist that the sect's interpretation of a way of life be followed closely in the college, and no one may interfere.

The representatives of the sect choose the president of the college, and the college has the freedom to choose its students. In some schools of this type, the intellectual life may be at a minimum, and freedom of expression on the part of faculty and students may be controlled. And although these schools form a striking contrast with many of the great universities and colleges in the United States, the two types exist side by side with complete independence.

But the personality of higher education in the United States is dominated by an even more important political fact and emotional attitude. In theory and generally in practice, the American college campus is open to everyone. The right to learning is one of the expressions of the strong American drive toward equality of economic and political condition, and the attempt to provide learning opportunities for millions has had an effect upon the quality of the education ultimately provided. The masses have been articulate about what product they expect from the colleges, and the colleges have been sensitive to the popular will. Now, they have had an indispensable function to perform. In every nation the institutions of learning play an important sociological role. In the United States the college plays a socializing role as being a major agency for introducing the young to the traditions and responsibilities of their society. American colleges, therefore, are not only institutions dedicated to the pursuit of learning. They have had to be communities with all the material and physical paraphernalia—and difficulties—of other human communities.

An understanding of the special emphasis in American colleges on providing a whole spectrum of services to students cannot be grasped only in terms of *anti-intellectualism*. They are also the results of an almost fervent belief in the advantages and potentialities of education on the part of the American public. This public has shown a willingness to support both private and public education to an extent never known before, and there is a desire on the part of almost every American father and mother that their children receive the maximum education available. These are factors to which American institutions of learning must respond. They express the vigor as well as the insecurity of a nation which had never recognized its strength and potential before World War I and which has not yet quite fully done so. There is still a residue of the frontier spirit in the United States, and both the fact of rigid social and economic stratification and a belief in its desirability are largely missing from the American scene. These are vital points to understand if one is to comprehend the complexities of higher education in the United States.

The American college student reflects the aspirations, the optimism, the unreality perhaps, of the fluid society from which he comes. He feels that he is free to move up the ladder to wealth and prominence; he is free to choose his mate and profession. And he also feels, perhaps, a peculiar need to belong to a community that has more than a common love of ideas to bind it together.

De Tocqueville observed many years ago the American passion for joining organizations and participating in public, political, and social affairs. He saw these peculiar American propensities as manifestations of the democratic spirit, of the conviction that each man was as good as his neighbor and thus entitled to mix fully in all aspects of public life. But one of the prices of equality, said de Tocqueville, was the loneliness. The equalization process erects impersonal mass models, which motivate Americans to join with their fellows in public and social endeavor in an attempt to escape their feeling of isolation.

Thus the keynote of the social life of American colleges is informality, but informality usually within firmly established social groups. The hardy quality of the fraternities, sororities, social clubs, eating clubs, honor societies, professional fraternities, and clubs of varying hues is significant. For many students they represent a kind of continuity and stability which they have not before experienced.

III

The administrator of an American college is faced with many problems; and the services offered to students, the extent of these services, and their place in the total educational scene are among the foremost. These are issues of policy and must be settled by the administration; they concern the aim and destiny of the institution and the means by which its goals are to be reached. If the administration has decided with clarity and depth of understanding its aim and destiny, then the dean of students, his staff, and the students will comprehend their roles in the institutional plan. But certain imperatives are clearly difficult to avoid.

Once the college assumes the obligation for the housing and day-to-day lives of its students, a special relationship is created which also places upon the college the responsibility for the health and well-being of its ctiizens. It is in the effort to fulfill this responsibility that the college has felt compelled to provide the student with health facilities, clubhouses, counseling, and many other services.

The provision of these services invariably entails additional administrative problems, and their judicious and efficient application takes the college administration along the paths of personal counseling and guidance. Morals, ethics, and politics, as well as hygiene and social skills are not academic subjects; they inescapably intrude into our daily lives.

If intellectual refinement could be achieved in an ideal environment where the mind could be freed from the burdens of the physical body, the attainment of learning would be a far different problem. Students are, however, Aristotelian political men, who cannot escape the social responsibilities of the community in which they find themselves or the physical nature of their being.

The formal pattern for the college's services is unimportant; but the recognition that the college has responsibilities to give such services has seemed apparent to most of those who have the ultimate responsibility for the shape of American education. To be sure, it must not be thought that everyone associated with American colleges sees the problem in the same way. At one extreme there are the Nestors to be found in most faculties who think that services to students, particularly counseling services, represent an undesirable form of coddling. At the other extreme there are the eager young psychologists and addicts of objective testing devices who see uses for their services everywhere. When an institution fails to define its responsibilities to provide services to its students precisely and thoughtfully, the result can be a sort of schizophrenia in administration.

Yet enlightened administrators have distilled a few conclusions to which broad recognition is now given. As most freshmen come from a diversity of secondary schools and are products of a young and often brash culture, they are socially immature and unevenly prepared for the college experience. In housing the younger students, colleges have recognized a responsibility and an opportunity for extending the educational program to meet the requirements which such circumstances impose.

The gulf between the application of this principle at an Eastern men's college and a coeducational, church-related college in Mississippi is so great that the principle itself might seem to be entirely different. But in reflecting the mores of the communities from which the students of these respective types of college come, they are alike. Yale, for example, has its beautiful houses, provided through the generosity of Mr. Harkness, where eminent faculty members live and commune intellectually with the residents of the houses. Rising Faun has its dormitories with a set of rules which may reflect a stern and inflexible code of morals. Yet it also puts its stamp upon its graduates, many of whom become useful and influential citizens. And both institutions recognize that they must install their students in an intimate community and must in some way stand *in loco parentis* to them. There is no wholesale answer to how this function can best be performed, for circumstances differ. But it is not a function which, given American circumstances, can be disregarded.

But there is a final question which must also be faced. Do the services American colleges provide their students advance or retard their progress? Does the extracurricular side of college life have educational value?

My eleven years as Dean of Students at the University of Chicago and my frequent visits to other colleges convince me that today I could answer my French friend, even more firmly, "*Oui, c'est important.*" Two world wars have markedly affected both the size and the quality of higher education in the United States. In the process, the field of counseling and service has grown in importance, although its leaders are still searching anxiously for the proper answers to the questions before them.

The American college pattern has taken deep roots, and the concept of services to students has become an integral part of this tradition. It is my sincere belief that the pattern which has evolved is consonant with the tone and quality of American life. The college scene, like the general scene, is never static in the United States. University scholars are constantly working to improve the intellectual level of our institutions; pure research is more generally recognized and more adequately rewarded than at any time in our history. Similarly, dedicated men and women in the personnel field are constantly seeking better methods of unobtrusively assisting undergraduate students to develop their latent talents. This is the primary objective of intelligent personnel workers. In most cases, I believe that they are succeeding.

8.

The Meeting of Minds and

the Making of the Scholar

SIGMUND NEUMANN
Professor of Government
Wesleyan University

The periods which have been known as "the crossroads of mankind" have always been the periods for the meeting of inquisitive, seeking minds. This has been true throughout history. It is a truth that is doubly pertinent in our own time of accelerated change and exchange.

It was such a crucial crossing of different intellectual currents that made the Renaissance the period in which the great awakening of modern Western man as we know him took place. This historical encounter of East and West led to the discovery and rebirth of Europe's own character and quality. For it confronted her with forces that came from a contrasting world which had previously been outside the European ken.

We are again living in such a period of open frontiers, which will force the different cultures of the world to recognize the values and concepts by which they live and to test them anew in the light of ideas and perspectives that come to them from abroad and afar.

I. TODAY'S WANDERING SCHOLARS

It is against this background that the essential contribution of the Fulbright scholars, this century's *fahrende Scholaren*, should be measured. The experience of the Fulbright scholars may well be a first step toward marking the potential new frontiers of this global age. It can lead us, indeed, to redefine and revitalize the university and its proper place in our society.

Such a reevaluation is of vital import. In this era of pressing specialization and professionalization, the scholar has all too often lost his classic function of professing the central traditions of his time and culture. The image of the scholar has been blurred in the public view and even within his own professional domain. His original calling has been caricatured. The scholar—the persistent crystallizer of his community's life forces and the promoter of their universal realization—is now stereotyped instead as the provincial, absent-minded, and remote professor, who has lost contact with, and therefore impact on, his society. But the scholar, like any other meaningful social phenomenon, must be defined in time and space, and he must prove his mettle in the midst of the world he occupies. Hardly any period in history could give a more telling testimony to the always crucial role of the scholar than our own century, in which our civilization has been tested in the fate of our intelligentsia and their institutions, the universities. All too often, unhappily, the intelligentsia and their universities have been found wanting.

I come from a country that has the reputation of being the cradle of scholars. I left Germany after having tragically experienced the way in which this reputedly secure world of lasting wisdom and humane civilization caved in and collapsed overnight before the brutal onslaught of that curse of our time, modern totalitarianism. I am perhaps more than usually aware, therefore, of the dangers in an academic ivory tower which, like France's ill-fated Maginot line, can imprison its people behind its seemingly safe walls and can be swept away in the stream of barbarian movements.

When the Nazi revolution seemed to uproot everything—home, profession, national ties, the whole Western tradition and its moral code—life in the United States proved to be for me not only a chance for a new beginning, but also a test of a renewed dedication to all fundamental beliefs in man, society, and perennial values. By good fortune my personal migration coincided with a historic shift in international relations which called the United States—a nation composed of many nations—to world responsibility. Only the future can tell what the lasting impact will be of a cultural migration which, as a consequence of the Old World's revolutionary upheavals and radical persecutions, brought experienced European learning to these shores. But it seems more than possible that this migration has released a process of borrowing and assimilation, an exciting spiritual transfer, which may prove to be a significant turning point in the development of our modern civilization. Certainly it would not be the first time that the wanderings of displaced scholars have led to a firm rerooting of intellectual forces. The proud record of the Huguenots and their lasting influence through the ages offers ample testimony of what such migrations can mean.

The role of the wandering scholar in our time, however, is not reserved only to those who settle permanently in a new environment (and in this sense stop wandering). It refers even more to the happier two-way traffic which our expanding exchange activities have fostered. It is this program, its promise and perils, which is our concern in this essay. The value of these intensified exchanges for the furthering of international understanding is widely recognized. But it may be worth considering what these new experiences in international exchange mean to the scholar himself and the world in which he lives.

Viewing the United States and its world of scholars against such experiences, one gains a new, refreshing, and encouraging insight into our educational landscape. "To know thyself, compare thyself to others." Goethe's dictum most certainly applies well to our knowledge and understanding of national institutions. It is not accidental that the most penetrating and lasting accounts of the United States (as of any other peoples) were written by visitors from foreign lands, such as de Tocqueville and Lord Bryce, who incidentally returned home with a deeper understanding of their own nation's plight and position: the double reward of a round trip well completed.

Such *Wanderjahre* were the capstone of a young nobleman's completed education in the seventeenth and eighteenth centuries which ushered in an enlightened civilization. It brought about the beginning of a truly international community of scholars. What happened in these past periods as the exceptional experience of a selected set of young aristocrats—and for this reason was prepared, executed, and followed up with greatest care and circumspection—has become a daily occurrence in this age of transcontinental travels. Yet the fruits of such transactions may well be forfeited if they are not preserved and protected against the spoilage of flighty flings and rough handling.

II. HAZARDS AND HANDICAPS

It may well be appropriate to make a careful check of the dos and don'ts, of the promise and perils, of international exchange in our time. *Wenn jemand eine Reise tut, dann kann er was erzählen* (When somebody is making a journey, then he can tell quite a story)—as the old song goes. But does he tell the right story? Does he get the proper view? Does he really open his eyes to new impressions? Or will he simply return from his Cook's tour with his preconceptions reinforced and with more assurance than ever about the superiority of home sweet home? If this is the case, he might have stayed right on his old Main Street and saved himself the trouble of the trip. In an age in which international travel is becoming so much more easy, we face the peril of a world populated by bored parasites, running in all directions in the search after bigger and better escapes from their own native habitats—a world in which everybody is going someplace but nobody knows where he stands. How can a meaningful international exchange program prevent banal busybodies and superficial world tourists, who collect world-wide travel impressions as hunters collect moose heads, from becoming the scourge of our restless century?

The Fulbright program must stand or fall on the setting of correct criteria. Obviously the intelligent choice of candidates is the first safeguard against the pitfalls that have been described. The agencies that must select the ideal ambassadors abroad have the primary responsibility. Their task is not made easier by the fact that a Fulbright application has now become something like a badge of status for most self-respecting senior scholars. Boards of Selection are now in a position similar to that of the harassed college admissions officers in the United States who must pick and choose among hordes of eager applicants. But even if the right choices are made—and by and large this seems to be the case—there still remain a host of hazards and handicaps. Once the prospective wandering scholar has been chosen, his likely difficulties may come from one or both of two main sources—place and time.

One might do well to recall the careful preparation for a gentleman's tour abroad that took place in former centuries, a preparation that helped give shape to an earlier international society. Letters of introduction to well-chosen persons in each community that was visited opened the proper doors and thus assured a warm welcome and an enriching experience. By contrast how often are our visitors pitched into the wrong places and directed to the wrong levels? A steady stream of visitors to centers of learning has led many institutions, in the effort simply to protect themselves, to develop a set of relay stations for the routinized processing of the perpetual passers-by—much to the dismay of everyone concerned. Years of experience should convince us that the law of diminishing returns applies here as elsewhere. The mounting quantity of callers naturally diminishes the quality of their reception. Moreover, the preferred and respected meccas of intellectual life in our time have all too often become Grand Central Stations where the traffic congestion is intense. They do not offer the conditions that are the prerequisites of a visitor's genuine appreciation of a strange environment: hospitable intimacy and reflective repose.

The small islands of intensive intellectual exchange, those little universities and colleges that are off the beaten path of organized travel tours and lack the glamour of world renown, may promise a more rewarding stay for the foreign scholar both in the United States and elsewhere. They often reflect a truer image of a nation than the more frequented metropolitan centers which, indeed, begin to look more and more alike with their up-to-date airports, chromium hotel lobbies, streamlined avenues, cocktail conversations, cosmopolitan entertainment, and fashionable patterns of thought.

Of course, such a diversion of the steady stream of visiting scholars from the customary channels will demand much more directed and continuous planning than we are usually willing to give to these efforts at international bridge building. Moreover, exclusive residence at even well chosen centers may easily give a misleading picture of a nation's over-all character. To counteract such limited vista it becomes increasingly essential to top off an intensive residence at *one* spot with a confrontation of the host nation's wider aspects and aspirations through additional travels and contacts.

Probably one of the most promising projects in this respect has been the Fulbright Conferences which bring foreign scholars from many lands at the end of their stay in the United States together with a group of American colleagues in extended and informal sessions on a friendly campus. It is hard to tell which side gains more from those encounters. The hosts not only sometimes detect and, perhaps, dispel the visitors' accumulated perplexities, but they also learn to articulate for the benefit of their guests the essentials of their own plight. This provides a chance at self-education which is rarely realized in the enclosure of one's private existence. The returning travelers, on the other hand, receive a more balanced and comprehensive view of their trip abroad. Such a reorientation—as important at the end of the tour as orientation conferences at the beginning—seems to be a *must* for a successful sojourn.

Equal consideration must be given to the factor of time if favorable results in the exchange program are to be achieved. One might suggest only half jokingly that a "disarmament period" of at least one-half year's duration is required in order to assure a suitable attitude of ready reception on the part of the visitor; for he does not enter his host country empty-handed and cannot easily drop his ballast on arrival. On the contrary, his preconceived prejudices may seek quick confirmation on his first encounter. Alas! many a visitor writes (or at least conceives) his travelogue immediately on arrival, when he is not hampered by facts and afterthoughts; and he may be prone to stick to these initial impressions, which have in fact originated long before he set foot in the new land. We live by national stereotypes—derived from the movies, hearsay, or simple ignorance—of the proverbial Chinese laundryman, of German generals looking and acting like Baron von Stroheim, and of the Paris of Josephine Baker's *Follies*. It takes time to part from accustomed images.

A short stay in a new country, therefore, is usually useless and sometimes even dangerous. A year seems to be the minimum period needed for a visit to make a dependable impression on the mind. The longer and more intensive the exposure in a given setting, the more assured seems to be an accurate account. The maxim, therefore, should be: "Stay put to get a long range view!" And on top of that, a repeat performance may give the finishing touch. It is not accidental that visitors from abroad, especially those from the British Isles, may do better on a return trip. For this permits the solidifying of the first tour's impressions, now filtered through the sharpened vista of one's own home base and refocused on second sight.

Indeed, time is needed to set and digest experiences. The delayed action of a creative intermission may often be the necessary agent to bring the full returns and lasting effects of the scholar's foreign sojourn.

III. SCHOLAR'S GROWTH AND SOCIETY'S GAIN

What do these provisos amount to? No more and no less than the realization that cultural exchange must be seen as a complex process of reorientation if it is to be a useful instrument for the scholar's growth and society's gain.

What should the scholar expect to get out of his extended itinerary? While he may put it on top of his agenda, professional proficiency is probably the least important result. In this age of world communication this aim can be attained—though, of course, not so well—through the established channels of regular scholarly publications, international learned conferences, and specific short visits. An extended trip abroad, in fact, is likely to mean a rude interruption of organized research in the familiar surroundings of one's own laboratories and libraries. Certainly it takes time to reestablish similarly favorable conditions in a new setting, if it is possible at all. But this is, of course, only rarely the main purpose of the tour, any more than is the acquisition of special skills and techniques. The magic of new gadgets has played havoc wtih many exchange programs.

The real reward of the scholar's interrupted routine comes in the opening of new vistas and in the reorientation of his accustomed position. What an international exchange promises is a truly liberal education. There is, first of all, the exciting comradeship of the international community of scholars. "A fig tree looking on a fig tree becometh fruitful," as an old Arab proverb goes. And there is no national borderline to this experience. The cross-fertilization of ideas has been the accepted pattern for cultural and intellectual development since the founding of the great universities in thirteenth-century Europe. When statesmen, interest groups, and even religious organizations are caught in the net of national commitments, the world fraternity of scholars may well be one of the most potent forces we have to promote international good will.

Moreover, scholar meets scholar on a most personal plane. If international understanding is to be realized as something more than a pious prayer or an abstract generalization, it must take shape in the minds of living men who are involved in common purposes. The identity of scholarly pursuits establishes a natural base for such understanding. Human bonds grow almost automatically as by-products of the meeting of men with mutual interests. Such indirect methods make for better international understanding than the more direct methods which missionaires for "one world" may adopt.

The same goes for a full appreciation of a national civilization. The young scholar who, from the vital center of his own scholarly domain, reaches out for enriching experiences, may register with greater ease the life forces of a nation than the professional pulse taker of international good will. Of course, such incidental bridge building presupposes the light touch and ready hand of a student who is young, at least in heart, and thus open to suggestion. But then international exchange naturally concentrates on the maturing professional who has the main part of his career before him. And that applies to his role as an exchange scholar, too.

The Fulbright program is set up as a two-way traffic. It

definitely does not end with the trip abroad. It is a lifelong mission, if properly conceived. In fact, the really difficult task begins on the return from foreign lands, when one has to fit the experiences abroad into a useful pattern at home. This effort often constitutes a complex process of rerooting and reconditioning. Far too little attention is given to this crucial stage which frequently attests to the success of the exchange program and— like so many peace settlements, spoiling the fruits of victory—it may be lost if one is not fully alerted to the perils of the aftermath.

Two reactions, seemingly contradictory and yet not altogether unrelated, persistently prevail among those who have returned: nostalgia and bitterness. Homesick for paradise lost, the wandering scholar may first of all try to prolong his stay abroad and, if that fails, to pursue plans for an early return. A good part of this desire may simply be ascribed to the exaltations of an experienced past, a holiday when one was free from the daily grind of commitments at the home base. Such a morning-after feeling is the familiar price paid for a sabbatical leave.

Yet the Fulbright scholar's troubles may go deeper. His hosts may have done almost too good a job, by making him feel at home abroad to a point of detesting the conditions he is to meet at his regular post. Interestingly enough, it is often the student who originally rejected the new experience who falls hardest for his host country. His new love may be discovered in a delayed reaction only when he hits the home ground again. Whatever the reason for such a reaction, and whenever it may set in, it definitely defeats the purposes of international exchange. Meant to enrich the returning student for fruitful functions awaiting him in his own country, travel should not end in a sense of frustration at home and in a craving for an early return to the fields one has visited.

What has happened in this case is an alienation instead of a liberation of the wandering scholar. Such a result may have dire consequences and, in fact, can lead to the very opposite effects from those which an international exchange program is set up to have. The eventual result may even be a sharp rejection of the host country and all that it stands for. This unfortunate turn is not reserved only to the few "incorrigibles", who never wanted to open their minds to new experiences anyway and who should not have been sent abroad in the first place. It is a serious peril among people who, in a not infrequent pattern of love turning to hatred, turn against an initially appreciated foreign experience and try to eradicate it from their affections altogether. In this way they seek to free themselves from disturbing influences that make them feel no longer at home on their native ground.

This strange and unfortunate phenomenon should not be written off simply as the proverbial ingratitude with which human beings are prone to pay for the favors they have received. It is part of a process (perhaps subconscious) of self-defense against a sense of alienation which often grows in individuals who return to their homes after a prolonged absence.

Accordingly, if one does not fully understand the perplexities of transcontinental acculturation, the consequences can be disastrous and far from those that are intended.

There are three stages in the development of a "Fulbright experience", and all three are essential to a satisfactory outcome: the selective preparations at the start, the experience in the host country, and the follow-up after the scholar's return. The scholar sent abroad may not leave with a definite marching route and clearly circumscribed assignments, but he certainly must be assured of his place and function at home when he is to return. This orientation toward his future role must be constant while he is away. Not accidentally are those visitors the most successful ones who know that their collected experiences will be used fully on their return and who are directed, therefore, by a purposeful drive even while they roam widely abroad.

The host country also has a responsibility to reinforce and redirect the future home assignments of the visitor. Instead of overselling its riches (in a natural though misplaced pride in its achievements), the host country has to probe into the requirements of its visitor and help him in the discovery of useful material for his own urgent tasks. It should be as eager to learn from its guest as it is to impart to him something of its own experience and traditions.

Accordingly, rich and satisfactory association between a visitor and his hosts requires that both sides pay attention to the importance of understanding not only the other's country but the other's position. The host who would lend a helping hand to the scholar from abroad must possess not only a wide knowledge of other peoples and a high degree of tact and sensitivity, but should also understand what life was like at home for the visitor whom he is initiating into a new country. Conversely, the visitor must learn something not only about the facts of life in the country he is visiting and not only about the problems of being a host, but also about his own basic perspectives and expectations. If he is unaware of where he himself stands, it is unlikely that he will quite comprehend where others stand and why they do so. Grandiose blueprints for world-wide improvements and generalizations about the similarities of human beings in all parts of the world will not produce the sort of concrete understanding and personal sympathy on which the exchange program ultimately depends. It may also be important that the host remind himself that the visiting scholar will be aided in orienting and distilling his impressions if he is given a chance, shortly before his departure, to assess them in the light of his future work when he returns home.

Finally, the success of the exchange program will also depend in large part upon the reception which the visiting scholar receives when he returns home. He may have to undergo a period of painful readjustment similar to that experienced when he first started his tour. He may even have to counteract the prejudices of his neighbors against the traveler who has "fallen for foreign ways." If the scholar who has returned can fit his experiences into a well-defined position, which had been clearly assigned him before he left his country, many of these difficulties can be considerably diminished. Indeed, it is the individual who is well rooted in his own country who can serve best as a living link between two nations and an interpreter of each to the other. By responding to such an opportunity, such an individual will not only widen his countrymen's horizons but will have an added dedication to his own fate and function at home. Such a continuing service to the cause of international exchange could be reinforced by the organization of communities of former Fulbright scholars. It might also be worth consideration to renew invitations to take part in the exchange program, after a lapse of five years or so, to those scholars who have proved themselves to be continuing representatives of its purposes.

For any great social enterprise, what counts in the end is the readiness of devoted individuals to commit themselves to it in a lasting fashion. In *A Bell for Adano*, John Hersey's moving report of the efforts of a Major Victor Joppolo in the American military government in Italy, Hersey writes, "No Charter, no Four Freedoms or Fourteen Points, no dreamer's diagram so symmetrical and so faultess on paper, no plan, no hope, no treaty —none of these things can guarantee anything. Only man can guarantee, only the behavior of men under pressure, only our Joppolos." It is in such an encounter of man and man that the overwhelming and insurmountable tensions of international conflict can find concrete, even if only temporary, solutions. This

9.

Conclusion: Critical Issues
in American Higher Education

CHARLES FRANKEL
Professor of Philosophy
Columbia University

The essays in this volume have described where American higher education now stands. But they have done something more. They have raised questions about where American higher education ought to go. For, as the foregoing essays suggest, there is one fact about the present situation of American colleges and universities which probably overshadows all the others: it is the widespread feeling that the American system of higher education is under stress. Throughout the United States colleges and universities are engaged in extensive reappraisals of their programs. The public is generally concerned and the attention of government has been focused on the question as well. Indeed, for the first time in a long while, the quality and goals of American higher education, and not only its availability and its cost, have become explicit political issues. The present generation of American teachers and scholars is plainly confronted by a series of difficult choices.

The choices arise, as the essays by Professors Sanders, Strozier, Franklin, and Brode indicate, out of the changing demands that American society makes upon its higher educational institutions. And they arise as well, as Professors McKeon, Oppenheimer, and Ulich have pointed out, because American universities are twentieth-century universities and have problems to settle about their own changing traditions and bodies of knowledge, and about the goals of education itself. No one actively engaged in teaching and scholarship in an American university can be without views and preferences on such issues. On the theory that it is pleasanter to be hanged for the crimes that one confesses than for the crimes that others only suspect, I shall make no effort to hide such opinions as I may have and shall try to suggest where I think the right answers lie. But my main purpose is not to advocate certain solutions. It is to draw together the main themes that have been touched on in this volume and to indicate those persistent facts of life in the United States which may help us to see American educational problems in their context and to understand why they are what they are.

How have these problems arisen? Despite what must sometimes seem to be the case, they have not arisen because American education has invented them. As Professor Neumann intimates, the scholar who visits these shores cannot help but be struck by those features of American colleges and universities that mark them off most sharply from the educational institutions he knows at home. He will notice that research in American universities often seems less individualistic and more highly organized, that universities are more busily administered and more urgently and nervously "sold" to the public, that American students seem to be more closely supervised, more elaborately protected, more vigorously exercised, and more solemnly prayed over. Professor Sanders has spelled out the various ways in which scholarship has been organized in the United States to serve the needs of the community. President Strozier has indicated how broadly the colleges of America construe the meaning of the term *education* and how elaborately they undertake to educate their students in almost all the meanings of the term.

All this may seem to the visiting scholar to be the reflection of a consistent and deliberate philosophy. And he will be encouraged to draw this conclusion by the constant discussion of educational philosophies that marks the American scene, and by the slogans —"education for democracy," "training the whole man," "making citizens"—with which almost every public discussion of education in the United States seems condemned to begin and end. The United States is the only major nation in the world whose national identity was originally defined by a declaration of abstract principles. It is perhaps natural, therefore, that Americans should have the habit of explaining their behavior as though it were the acting out of a conscious creed. But this habit can mislead the foreign observer almost as much as it misleads Americans themselves.

Philosophies of education may guide American teachers and scholars in choosing among the alternatives that confront them. But these philosophies are not responsible on the whole for the fact that these alternatives are what they are. American higher education is a social institution, like religion, the state, or the property system, and its problems originate in the same way problems originate in these other institutions. They arise out of discordant traditions, out of internal conflicts of interest and external collisions with other institutions, out of the emergence of new needs and new resources, and, broadly, out of the interplay of human ideas and ideals with the refractory conditions of human nature and the social and physical environment. Americans do have theories of education, and these theories do raise problems—and sometimes eyebrows. But in the main the problems of American higher education have not arisen because Americans have deliberately chosen to act in one way and not in another; they are not problems that have arisen from putting a specific philosophy of education into practice. They have emerged out of stubborn imperatives on the American scene, imperatives that would in all likelihood be present, philosophy or no philosophy. A philosophy of education may deal with such imperatives reasonably or unreasonably; it may convert them into opportunities or moan over them as immovable obstacles; but it does not create them.

The facts of life that pose the issues that are now critical in American higher education, furthermore, are not, on the whole, of recent vintage. It is tempting to think that the questions that bedevil one's own generation are new and unprecedented, and in approaching the current problems of American universities it is easy to imagine that they are merely contemporary. But this is not the case. In their main lines the issues that are critical in American higher education today, I am inclined to think, are issues come to a focus that have existed for a century or more. And it may be helpful to look at current problems in this long-range perspective.

The questions that have been raised by the authors of this volume, it seems to me, reflect three fundamental and persistent issues with which almost every generation of American scholars and teachers must apparently wrestle. The first is the problem of harmonizing the disparate traditions out of which American higher education springs and of domesticating them within a mobile and democratic society. The second is the problem of finding the sort of moral and financial support for American scholarship that will permit it to maintain its freedom and standards. The third is the problem of establishing a sound relationship between a technologically oriented culture and the institutions and ideals of pure science and disinterested inquiry.

I

American higher education has a mixed ancestry. At the under-graduate level, it is mainly Anglo-Saxon in its background; at the graduate and professional levels, it is primarily Continental in its traditions. The diverse orientations which this mixed ancestry has produced are the source of one of the persistent issues in American higher education—the discontinuity between under-graduate and graduate education.

Anglo-Saxon education is a complicated phenomenon, but its distinctive characteristics can be stated fairly briefly. Its objectives are moral as well as intellectual, and it seeks the growth of the student in character as well as in knowledge and skills. It conceives education, therefore, as a function of a planned environment which includes a good deal more than classroom arrangements. In the classic British or American college, the student lives in a home away from home, where, in a carefully controlled situation, he has an opportunity to live and work with his peers as though—or almost as though—he were an adult. His college attempts to provide him with a protected and purified microcosm of the larger world. In this imitation world the student is placed in a series of rehearsal situations in which he can play seriously, as it were, at the kind of thing he is going to do as an adult. He reads and writes, of course, and receives training in the learned disciplines. But he also joins dramatic groups and literary societies, works on student newspapers, or takes part in student athletics. His interests and his energies are focused predominantly on the college scene, and it is expected that he will find within the college a training ground for almost anything he wishes to do.

In contrast with the Continental student, then, the American undergraduate has traditionally been a relatively insulated creature. He is deliberately kept *in statu pupilare;* and, ideally, that status embraces the whole of his life. Thus, unlike students in Paris or Cairo, the American student's political activities, for example, are unlikely to take place in the streets of great cities. In the thirties, to be sure, the political activities of American students began to look like the activities of students elsewhere in the world. But for the most part, American students, though they have a strong interest in politics, have been mainly interested in their own politics. Their energies have gone into the activities of student political parties and student government. These have most of the rhetoric and trappings of American politics at large. They differ, indeed, in only two respects. The issues are small and few are permanently hurt. They are cushioned rehearsal situations.

In sum, the American college, with its Anglo-Saxon background, leans towards a student-oriented, rather than a subject-oriented, education. Subjects are taught; but for the most part the announced reason for doing so is that they are means to the development of the individual. Different colleges, of course, strive to attain this goal in different ways, as Professor Ulich has indicated. Antioch College differs from Sarah Lawrence; both are at the opposite pole from St. John's College in Annapolis; and all three differ from Amherst or Swarthmore. But despite the vigorous debates which these different approaches provoke, almost all American colleges are likely to seem to an outside observer to express a strikingly similar conception of their ultimate purpose. Their function, they believe, is to bring out the best in the individual student by providing him with something like a planned and total environment. The services to students which Dr. Strozier has sketched are part of this effort.

But this is the undergraduate side of the picture. When we turn to the graduate and professional divisions of the typical American university, we move to an educational environment that bears a much closer resemblance to the Continental scene. The graduate student, or the student in schools of medicine or law, is on his own. Beyond providing him with a place to reside and a few of the amenities, the university, on the whole, contents itself with giving him a formal education; he must get his informal education where he can. He is in an institution which is interested in students, but interested in them mainly because they are instruments for preserving a discipline or a profession. There are graduate and professional schools in the United States, to be sure, which proudly proclaim that they "teach students, not subjects," and which provide widely diversified programs of instruction adapted to the interests of different individuals. But even such schools must admit in the end that it is their function to teach not just individuals as individuals, but men and women who will become doctors, social workers, economists, or philologists.

Like its counterparts in most other parts of the world, then, the American graduate school is in the last analysis an institution that differs sharply from the American college. It is not of and for students; it is of and for professional scholars. The scholar teaches because teaching is an instrument for testing and publishing his ideas, and because it is a necessity if the subject he loves is to be carried on by others. What really counts for him is the maintenance of the traditions and standards of his discipline and the extension of the area of knowledge it commands.

The difference between undergraduate and graduate education, of course, is a difference in emphasis, not an absolute difference in kind. The graduate teacher with a complement of normal emotions cannot be indifferent to the human beings in front of him; and despite the popularity of the slogan in undergraduate colleges that "one teaches students not subjects," it is obvious that one does not teach a student by teaching him nothing and that the undergraduate teacher who cares about teaching is likely to care about his discipline as well. Nevertheless, as most students who have made the transition will confirm, there is frequently a profound difference between an American student's experience as an undergraduate and his experience as a student in a graduate or professional school. There is a difference in atmosphere, and in basic attitudes toward the purpose of intellectual training, that separates most American graduate and professional schools from the colleges from which their students come. And this difference is the source of deep divisions and tensions within the American educational community and, for that matter, within the individual scholars who compose it.

But American universities do not simply represent the continuation of older Anglo-Saxon and Continental traditions. They embody what happened to these traditions when they were transplanted to a new and different social scene. In at least two respects, both the American college and the American graduate and professional school have had to meet educational needs that neither the traditional Anglo-Saxon nor the Continental university had to meet.

American schools from kindergarten through high school have not had simply to transmit knowledge and skills. Professor Franklin's essay touches on a theme that is much larger than the immediate issue of desegregation. There has been steady pressure for the democratization of educational opportunity in the United States because education has been the principal instrument for the democratization of American life. Schools have been the major agencies in the United States by which a common experience has been given to American youth, and something like a unified culture has been formed out of the multitude of traditions from which the population of the United States springs. This is why the question of desegregation strikes so deep. And it is also why the theory flourishes in the United States, as it flourishes perhaps nowhere else in the world, that the school is itself a small society, and that its primary function is not to train the young in intellectual skills but in the habits and attitudes that will make them desirable members of the social group.

This theory has been carried so far in many quarters that it has been turned into something close to a caricature of itself. But whatever may be the present merits of this theory, it was at least initially a response to necessity. In many American schools the simple fact has been that it has not been possible to teach students fundamental intellectual skills until after they have first been taught a common code of manners and, indeed, a common language. The question whether the school is an agency for making citizens or for teaching reading, writing, and arithmetic is not in the United States simply an abstract issue. It is a difficult practical question. And the problem is not solved by the time American students reach college. Like American elementary or secondary schools, American colleges are also agencies for forming a culture and not merely for transmitting it; and even if they attempt to limit their purposes and to concentrate on purely intellectual training, they receive the graduates of a school system which has to meet a multitude of widely different demands.

But there is a still more significant function which American colleges and universities serve and which inevitably affects their educational programs. From a sociological point of view, the American college has one primary meaning. It is the great social escalator of contemporary American society, the major avenue by which the members of a mobile society are enabled to move upward on the social scene. Young Americans come to college to learn how to behave and how to dress; they come to college to meet—and to marry—the right people; they come so that they can leave labeled "college graduate." For the college degree is one of the few symbols of status that exists in the United States, and its social importance is all the greater as a result.

All this, of course, has an inevitable effect on what American colleges can and must do. American college students have two characteristics. The first is that most of them are newcomers to the environment of higher education. The second is that the majority of American students do not come to college out of a love of learning for its own sake. They come to improve themselves economically and socially, and their interest in their education is likely to be practical and vocational, often narrowly so. There are bound to be certain educational problems as a result. No matter what their philosophies of education, almost all American colleges have had to devote time to training their students in such elementary skills as English composition. And in one way or another they have also had to do something more. They have had to acquaint individual students with the existence —and the excitement—of a larger world of learning of which the student's own specialized interests are only a part. The so-called courses in "general education"—the surveys of history, literature, philosophy, or the problems of democratic citizenship—about which so much discussion can be heard in American educational circles are efforts to meet this need.

There is much to be said for and against these programs, but there are probably few in the United States who would say that American colleges have wholly succeeded in solving the problems from which such programs arise. But it is at least possible that American colleges have been dealing with an educational and intellectual issue that is likely to come increasingly to the foreground in higher education in the twentieth century in most parts of the world. The tradition of liberal education has been mainly an aristocratic tradition, and for most of its history its principal beneficiaries have come from the social classes that enjoyed inherited wealth, position, and a large opportunity for leisure. Among the Romans the liberal arts were the disciplines which it was deemed appropriate to teach those enjoying the legal status of free men; and until at least the end of the nineteenth century, liberal education was conceived as an education for men who, in the main, were *born* free men,—men, that is to say, who were not bound down by economic or social deprivation, men who did not need to work and had no impelling reason to wish to move out of the social class into which they were born.

In the United States, however, liberal education has for the most part been aimed at young men and women who do not come from a small and easily identifiable "ruling class." Most of the young men will remain ordinary citizens with moderate incomes; most of the young women will spend their most vigorous years as housewives and mothers; and now that the domestic servant has all but disappeared from American homes, these young women will devote a good part of each day to manual tasks. To initiate such students into the traditions of liberal scholarship is to attempt to give them a view of learning—and, indeed, a view of life—which is at least a little alien to their past experience and which is likely to collide with their daily routines in later life. It is a formidable task, and it requires a good deal more than tinkering with classroom techniques. It requires an effort of creative imagination in the classroom, and it also requires the reexamination of the liberal-arts tradition so that it will speak with some force and pertinence to the members of a democratic society.

The difficulty of the task, however, is proportionate to its importance. For, quite apart from social conditions, knowledge, discriminate taste, and the pursuit of learning are inherently aristocratic values. They can be enjoyed only at the price of arduous discipline, and if they could be bought cheaply—which is impossible—their excitement would be gone. No democratic culture will be better if its attachment to such values has been weakened. The more democratic American and world society becomes, and the more widely educational opportunity becomes available, the more pressing is the obligation of the contemporary university to maintain its commitment to these aristocratic ideals. And the greater is its obligation as well to communicate to students something of the ancient sense of the interdependence of the scholarly disciplines. When the educated classes of a society are made, not born, when they do not constitute a hereditary group whose members have always known each other in the same clubs or met at the same summer resorts, they do not normally enjoy the birthright of a common intellectual culture. If they are to have a common intellectual background, they must acquire it through formal schooling. The alternative—and, as

Dr. Oppenheimer has pointed out, it is a danger that faces any technically specialized contemporary society—is to produce a breed of intellectual leaders who cannot speak to one another, or to other men, across the walls of their specialties. Those who hope for intelligent leadership in modern society must surely aim at something more than the training of learned experts who are barbarians. What can be done about these issues as they are currently presenting themselves?

At present there are two dramatic instances in the United States of the sort of steady pressure which a democratic social environment puts on established patterns of education. The first of these has been discussed by Professor Franklin. It is the controversy over desegregation. Those who come from other societies that continue to be torn by ancestral conflicts will understand why this is not an issue that has been easy to solve. The moral issue, however, is unequivocally plain: American pronouncements about the evils of colonialism, it need hardly be said, sit very ill as long as the nonsense and the cruelty of racial doctrines persist in the United States. But it is partly because this moral issue has become so plain within the United States itself that it seems to me overwhelmingly probable, despite the bitterness and clamor that has been aroused, that educational segregation will be effectively eliminated in the United States within the coming generation.

But this issue, of course, is part of a larger, and in the long run even more significant development—the dramatic rise in the number of those who seek a higher education. This situation is in part the result of the simple increase in the size of the American population; but it is also the result of "the revolution of rising expectations" which characterizes the American scene as it has now come to characterize most other nations of the world. A larger and larger proportion of the American nation is coming to believe that the right to a higher education is included within the general right to the pursuit of happiness. Within the next two decades American colleges, if they maintain existing standards and admit the same proportion of those who apply, will have to take care of about twice as many students as they have in the past.

It is useful to be clear about one's values in facing a situation of this kind. It would be romantic to imagine that the principal reason for the increased demand for a college education in the United States is anything else than what it has usually been—the desire for money and social position. But these desires are old desires; and they are surely not more dishonorable than the motives which led the children of hereditary aristocracies to the universities in the past. And surely they are not incompatible with the serious pursuit of an education: they may, after all, help young men and women to apply themselves. Indeed, it seems to me a novel and happy event in the history of mankind that obtaining a higher education has become a main path to social position. It is an event at which university professors particularly ought to rejoice. Any society will be richer if it can give greater opportunities to the intelligent, wherever they are found. And one of the considerable moral achievements of the twentieth century is the growth of the simple conviction that every individual ought to have as much schooling as his talents permit. Wherever this conviction is growing it is creating educational problems, but it is difficult to believe that the world would be better without such problems.

Yet this is obviously only part of the issue. For it is either innocence or demagoguery to assert that we can continue to give the same kind of education that we have given in the past to this great number of students unless strict safeguards are erected. The obvious danger is that more and more Americans will be the holders of college degrees that mean less and less. And the danger is all the greater because American education has always been troubled by the tendency to practicalism and vocationalism, and by the temptations to simplify, to survey superficially, to cheapen, that arise in the process of translating the ancient culture of the liberal arts into terms that will be meaningful to a restless and impatient people.

Probably the most important practical measure that can be taken to meet this problem is to push farther in distinguishing between the educational missions of different types of colleges and universities. The two-year junior college, the technical school, the liberal-arts college for young men and women, the adult liberal-arts college, the municipal institution, and the great state university all serve their special functions; and, as Professor Sanders rightly emphasizes, the functions are complementary, not competitive. And beyond such institutions, some American colleges should make it their special business to train those who will go on to advanced work in the arts, sciences, and professions. Last, but not least, there should be institutions, both undergraduate and graduate, which are willing to limit the size of their student bodies and to stake their destinies on the principle that it is impossible to aim too high. The obligation to lift the intellectual level of large numbers has been the historical imperative that has shaped American higher education; but American higher education has an equal obligation to maintain the image and the ideal of intellectual excellence. Unless some institutions exemplify this ideal uncompromisingly, the pace and temper of the entire system of education will suffer.

Furthermore, changes are already taking place in the character of the American college student which make a great many traditional assumptions questionable. According to a report of the Commission on the College Student of the American Council on Education, reported in *The New York Times*, October 16, 1958, the sort of student who used to be regarded as an exception is now more and more the rule. Forty per cent of all American undergraduates are now more than twenty-one years old. Since 1953 the number of undergraduates between twenty-five and thirty-four years of age has increased by forty-seven per cent while those who are eighteen or nineteen years old have increased by only thirty per cent. Twenty-two per cent of all American college students are married; and while estimates vary, it seems a good guess that forty per cent of all undergraduates earn more than half their college expenses. If American colleges are to contain a large admixture of such students, the Anglo-Saxon ideal of a protected and insulated educational environment makes less sense than it once did. And the rise of the municipal college, the evening college, and the adult college throws an even greater strain on this classic conception of the nature and function of undergraduate education.

In all probability, of course, those colleges which most Americans will continue to regard as typical will be populated mainly by students in their late adolescent years. For such students many of the services which President Strozier has described will continue to have a rationale; for there is no alchemy by which the products of American homes and American secondary schools can be turned overnight into the sort of student for whom the atmosphere of a Continental university would be appropriate. Nevertheless, in the years to come, such students are likely to be rubbing shoulders with an increasing number of older classmates; they are likely to be in college only after a serious competition to win admission; and they may be in colleges where standards are stiffer and the going is rougher. The time is probably ripe, therefore, to reexamine the desirability of all the educational pillows on which American colleges rest their students' heads. The elaborate machinery of grades and credits, the courses that plan a student's reading page by page, the consuming extracurricular activities, the counseling services: there is surely a point beyond which all these become distractions from the main business of education. If American undergraduates were given a good deal more independence than many colleges now give them, it would be a first large step toward making undergraduate education in the United States a better preparation for advanced study.

The division between undergraduate and graduate education in the United States, in short, is much too sharp, and it has worked to the disadvantage of education at both levels. American colleges, despite certain traditional assumptions, will not damage the ideal of liberal education by making their programs less leisurely and eclectic and more seriously preparatory for advanced study. And American graduate and professional schools will not hurt the cause of advanced study by recognizing that it is not only the undergraduate institution that has an obligation to educate its students liberally. Those who have specialized skills, and particularly those who are the masters of the more abstract disciplines, occupy the decisive positions in contemporary society. Whether they know it or not, they do not make only technical decisions; they make the moral and social decisions that have the largest influence on the intimate lives of ordinary people. If it is an obligation of graduate and professional schools to train specialists, it follows that it is also their obligation to train men and women who are in touch with the values of civilized life and who are aware of the intellectual and moral context of their activities.

II

But these issues touch on another central and persisting issue in American higher education: the problem of finding the kind of financial and moral support within the American community that will permit universities to keep their freedom and to concentrate on their main objectives. The problem has been successfully solved in the past; but it arises in different forms in different periods and constantly has to be solved again.

There have been four main sources of financial support for American higher education in the past. The first has been income from endowment, which has traditionally been the main source of support of the most powerful private universities in the United States. The second has been taxes paid by the public, which have been the major, though not the sole, source of support of municipal colleges and state universities. A third source of support has been the tuition fees paid by students. State universities to some extent, and private colleges and universities to a much larger extent, depend on this form of income; and some private universities in the United States, which have relatively small endowments, depend on tuition income to a great extent. Fourth, grants from philanthropic foundations, usually given to advance a specific purpose of the foundation, have helped universities to make ends meet. Such grants are playing a larger and larger role in current educational financing. Finally, a new and significant form of financial support for universities has recently emerged. This is the income derived from special contracts for research which the university may make with private or public agencies. By far the most important source of such income is research sponsored by the federal government.

A large part of the present story of American university economics is told when the fact is reported that income from endowment is now playing a steadily declining role. The increasingly corporate structure of American business, the steeply graduated income tax, and the rise in the tendency to establish private philanthropic foundations have all affected the funds available to universities for new endowment; and inflation has cut into the value of the endowments they already possess. As a result, it has become increasingly necessary for endowed universities to lean more heavily on other sources of income, not the least of which is tuition fees paid by students.

The dangers in such a situation are evident. A university cannot depend mainly on income from tuition fees without running the risk of depreciating its intellectual currency. Apart from a larger effort that must be made to receive donations from individuals who can make moderate contributions, American colleges and universities will almost certainly have to make a systematic effort to receive support from private associations like corporations and trade unions, which represent the major centers of concentrated wealth in the United States today. Indeed, it is one of the educational tasks of the American college and university today to develop in such agencies an attitude that recognizes a permanent obligation to support higher education—and without any strings attached.

It is unlikely, however, that support from such quarters will be enough to maintain the independence of universities. Money alone is not enough to maintain such independence; the money must come from a variety of different sources, no one of which has a decisive role. This principle probably applies indirectly even to state universities. Their record with regard to academic freedom, which on the whole is excellent, is at least in part the result of the fact that the record of private universities sets a standard which they are under pressure to follow. In the case of the private universities, which are struggling to maintain their standards in the face of the decreasing power of their endowments, it is likely that economic support from foundations and government will play a steadily larger role. This process, indeed, is already well under way. Most of this support, however, has come in the shape of grants or payments for specific projects in education or research.

Such support has been indispensable. Without it, for example, few American universities in the years since World War II would have been able to afford the enormously expensive equipment that is now necessary for experimental work in nuclear physics. There is little evidence, furthermore, that this large-scale government support has affected academic freedom for the worse. The government has encouraged research not simply in practical areas but in the fundamental theoretical disciplines. For the most part, indeed, it has simply helped scholars to do what they wished to do. And it is almost needless to say that the foundations have shown at least equal respect for the integrity of scholarly inquiry.

Nevertheless, there are potential risks, though hardly insurmountable ones. There is the risk that the humanities will be skimped; there is the risk that new projects and global schemes will be supported at the expense of the established disciplines and the conventional but important work of the university; there is the risk that the interest of government and the foundations in research will create an even greater tension than now exists between the responsibility of the university for research and its responsibility for teaching. Not least, there is the danger that scholars will be turned aside from their own central business. The heart of free inquiry lies in the initiative which scholars exercise, not simply in coming to conclusions which they think are true, but in asking the questions they think important. There is, to be sure, an inertia in the academic community against which outside agencies like the foundations and government can exercise a valuable countervailing influence. But in addition to support for the new and experimental, the aid of foundations and government must obviously go as well to the standard activities of universities in education and research. And in the case of government aid, it seems to me that there would be fewer risks rather than more risks if present arrangements, under which government aid is given for specific projects, were converted into a general and permanent program of aid to higher education as such. The arrangements which have been made in Great Britain and elsewhere offer suggestions as to the way in which government aid programs can be administered while protecting the freedom of universities.

But if American higher education must lean more heavily than ever on widespread support from private individuals and associations and from public funds, then it is plain that the health of higher education in the United States depends on more than money. It depends on understanding and on a climate of opinion. And so we come to an issue about which a good deal has been said in recent years, both in the United States and in other countries—the position of learning and of the learned man in American culture. It is an issue on which both Professor Brode and Dr. Oppenheimer have touched.

Anti-intellectualism is neither a distinctively new nor a distinctively American phenomenon. We look back on Athens as the great source of Western rationalism, but it was in Athens that Socrates was condemned to drink the hemlock, and the charge against him, as I understand it, was that he was an intellectual. Anti-intellectualism, indeed, is a trait not entirely alien to intellectuals themselves. The scholar is rare who exercises impassive objectivity when his own ox is gored, and, as Julien Benda's *La trahison des clercs* reminded us some years ago, the challenge to the ideals of intellectual objectivity and honesty has come not only from those who are not intellectuals, but from professional intellectuals themselves. Anti-intellectualism is the Old Adam in man, and there are few individuals, and fewer societies, that can be sure they have got the Old Adam under control.

In the United States, however, there are certain special circumstances which tend to exaggerate Old Adam's appearance of importance. The social revolutions which created the republics and democracies of modern Europe, Africa, or Asia were in large part led and guided by members of the intellectual classes. When the American Republic was founded, the story was more or less similar. Jefferson, Madison, Franklin, and Hamilton were recognizable intellectuals on the European model. During the nineteenth century, however, many movements that led to the fur-

ther democratization of American society came out of the frontier West and were in conflict with traditions on the Eastern
seaboard. But the intellectuals of America during the nineteenth
century were mainly Eastern seaboard people, products of the
great Eastern universities. To some extent anti-intellectualism in
America has been mixed, therefore, with a hostility toward the
Eastern seaboard, toward the rich and powerful and conservative,
toward those with an Old World look about them. There has
thus been a complicating social element, a political animus, in
what we know as anti-intellectualism on the American scene.
And a political animus has again been present in recent years,
when a large number of American professors and intellectuals
have been identified with liberal political movements.

There is an even more fundamental circumstance, however,
which can lead to mistakes in assessing the strength of anti-
intellectualism in the United States. This is the fact that intellectuals do not cut the same public figure in the United States
that they do elsewhere in the world. But neither do farmers,
workers, or professional people in the United States quite re-
semble their counterparts in other countries, and the reason is
the same. It is the relative paucity of visible symbols of class
status. Not many Americans practice or expect elaborate forms of
social deference, and few habitually identify either themselves or
others in terms of membership in a particular social class. When
the visiting scholar notices, therefore, that American intellectuals
seem to receive less obvious deference than do intellectuals in his
own country, he is reacting to a social attitude that affects not
only intellectuals but others as well.

If intellectuals do not receive the same overt deference in the
United States that intellectuals may receive elsewhere, neither
do lawyers, doctors, government officials, factory managers, or
ballet dancers. And in fact empirical sociological surveys made
in recent years suggest that the academic profession may well be

one of the more highly respected professions in the United States. Apparently, the self-image of American professors, their own estimate of the attitudes that are held toward them, is at variance with the dominant attitudes that actually exist.

Nevertheless, despite what has been said, it is undeniable that terms like "egghead" and even "professor" have mixed connotations in the United States, and that when professors are attacked as a result of their political activities, they are attacked not simply for the political views they hold but for being intellectuals as such. The tendencies associated with the name of the late Senator McCarthy do not leave a pleasant memory, even though they were relatively short-lived, and even though there is little evidence that leading academic figures were frightened into silence or that leading universities retreated from their normal sturdy respect for the academic freedom of their teaching staffs. In a period in which American institutions of higher learning require the intelligent understanding and support of large numbers, it must be part of the university's normal business, therefore, to conduct a steady program of community education which makes vivid and intelligible the university's role as a center of free inquiry and criticism.

III

The economic and moral relationship of American universities to the society of which they are a part raises, however, a final issue. It is the issue on which Professor McKeon has dwelt at the beginning of this book—the relation of higher education to a technologically oriented culture. There is in the United States, as no one needs to be told, an extraordinary admiration of technological achievement, which has behind it a century's struggle in conquering a continent. This attitude is not simply a practical attitude, an expression of the desire to get rich quick. The love of machinery in the United States is a moral and esthetic attitude. It expresses an admiration for technology as a way of work, and it is akin to the feelings which lovers of the fine arts have when they confront work that has been done with inventiveness, conscientious craftsmanship, and technical mastery of materials. Technology, so conceived, is surely not inherently alien to a humane civilization.

Nevertheless, the technological orientation of American culture is the source of one of the issues that is at once most lasting and most immediately urgent in American education. It creates a problem in at least two ways. In the first place, a technologically oriented culture is likely to be marked by an attitude of impatience with what has been done in the past. Since the human past hardly merits our unqualified respect, this attitude seems to me a not wholly unhealthy one. But it nevertheless adds to the difficulty of one of the scholar's central tasks. For, as no scholar needs to be told, he has an obligation to communicate the importance of disciplines and values that transcend the problems of the immediate and urgent present.

There is, therefore, a persisting tension in higher education in the United States. On one side, a vigorous, skeptical technological society demands that learning come to grips with living problems; on the other side, scholarly traditions demand that disinterested inquiry for ideal ends not be submerged under the pressures of the present. The tension is not in itself unhealthy, for it can help to guard scholarship against the insularity, exoticism, or preciosity into which it can fall so easily. But as almost every contributor to this volume has said, it is equally a function of a university not to be completely contemporary. A university is one of the institutions by which a society retains some sense of proportion about its place in time. In a technological society it is particularly important that universities keep this obligation deliberately in mind.

The second aspect of the issue raised by technology is even

more fundamental. Strangely enough, the place of technology in American life has served to obscure and confuse the idea of science. American students, like the American public at large, are likely to think of science as organized gadgetry, as a recipe for making tools. But technology is not the same thing as theoretical science, as the reader of Dr. Oppenheimer's essay will already have discerned. Technology involves the application of knowledge to the practical improvement of human life; and only the sentimental or the callous can regard such an enterprise as vulgar or unimportant. But theoretical science seeks simply to find an order in experience, and the uses to which this enterprise can be put are by-products. The distinctive good at which science aims is what philosophers used to call a "final good:" it is the good of seeing how separate and disparate phenomena hang together and how an orderly intellectual passage can be made from one event to another.

The problem of educating American students in such a way that they understand the place of science among the liberal arts is thus one of the long-standing problems in American education. There is probably no educational issue of greater importance. The intellectual edifice which the theoretical sciences are building represents an achievement of modern civilization which compares favorably in splendor, subtlety, and disinterested devotion with the achievements of any civilization in the past. As long as a large proportion of even the best educated members of modern society are unable to understand the nature of this achievement or to share vicariously in its joys, modern culture will not have come to terms with its own best and noblest work. It is as though the cathedrals of the Middle Ages had all been kept from public view and had been open only to a small and esoteric group. The sort of isolation of the creative scientist from the rest of his community of which men like Dr. Oppenheimer speak is not an inevitable or incurable state of affairs. But it requires the development of programs of education in the sciences which will present them as imaginative creations that make it possible for human beings to find more meaning and order in their experience. The participation by scientists in the development of such programs is probably their major educational task in the immediate future.

IV

But it is time to conclude, and it may be well to conclude with an obvious remark. The issues with which the authors of these chapters have been concerned are issues that are critical in American higher education today. No great powers of clairvoyance are needed, however, to see that many of these problems are likely to affect other educational systems as well. The use of universities to provide the practical knowledge and to train the technicians that a society needs to fight its way into control of its physical environment is a phenomenon that is appearing in Asia and Africa. The story that Professor Sanders tells is a story that is being repeated, in one form or another, elsewhere in the world. The same is true of the story that Professor Franklin tells. The struggle to expand the range of educational opportunity, and to make higher education available to groups that have hitherto been excluded by arbitrary social or economic barriers, is a major feature of the social revolution that has been taking place in most Western countries since World War II. And as a consequence, the problems of vocationalism, of student counseling, even of "general education," have begun to emerge in other educational systems besides the American. The attempt to domesticate the traditions of learning in a democratic and technological environment can hardly be put down any longer as a peculiarly Yankee enterprise. In many respects, the experience through which American higher education has gone provides a sort of dress rehearsal for the problems with which other educational systems are likely to be involved in the years to come.

No nation's way of dealing with these problems can be taken as a model for other nations. There may be suggestions about what should be done—and, perhaps, horrible examples of what should not be done—which scholars who visit these shores will take home with them. But it is not a function of international exchange programs to encourage the massive transplanting of scholars or of educational ideas from one country to another. Indeed, it may well be that it is a major function of exchange programs simply to alert scholars to the idiosyncrasies of their own native environments. There is a saying that the fish is the last creature in the world to discover the existence of water. It is probable that he only makes the discovery when he finds himself on dry land.

Professor Neumann has indicated the variousness of the values which the exchange program serves. One may hope that it will help scholars—and, through them, those they teach—to look upon ways that are alien to their own with some sympathy and understanding. One may hope, too, that the exchange program will help those who take part in it to cherish what is different from their own way of life because it is different, and not a dull mirror image of what they have always accepted. But the exchange of scholars has as its immediate purpose simply the advancement of the common goals of the international community of scholars. And in the end those who come to teach and work in American universities are likely to find that the professional problems with which they are concerned are the problems with which their American colleagues are also concerned.

There are distinctive and special problems on the American educational scene. In the final analysis, however, they are the problems of teachers and scholars whose mission is the same as that of scholars anywhere. That mission is to keep the tradition of disinterested learning alive; to add to the knowledge possessed by the race; to keep some solid, just, and circumspect record of the past; and to use what knowledge, skill, and critical intelligence exists for the improvement of the human estate. This is the function of universities wherever they are permitted to attend to their own proper business. The American university is simply a member of the international community of universities that serves this ancient cause.

TEXAS A&M UNIVERSITY TEXARKANA